CU00664320

VULNERABLE PEOPLE, VULNERABLE STATES

Over five decades of economic and technical assistance to the countries of Africa and the Middle East have failed to improve the life prospects for the more than 1.4 billion people who remain vulnerable. Billions of dollars have been spent on such assistance and yet little progress has been made. Persistent hunger and hopelessness threaten more than individuals and families. These conditions foster political alienation that can easily metastasize into hostility and aggression. Recent uprisings in the Middle East are emblematic of this problem. Vulnerable people give rise to vulnerable states.

This book challenges the dominant catechism of development assistance by arguing that the focus on economic growth (and fighting poverty) has failed to bring about the promised "convergence." Poor people and poor countries have clearly not closed the gap on the rich industrialized world. Pursuing convergence has been a failure. Here the authors argue that development assistance must be reconstituted to focus on creating *economic coherence*. People are vulnerable because the economies in which they are embedded do not cohere. The absence of economic coherence means that economic processes do not work as they must if individual initiative is to result in improved livelihoods. Weak and vulnerable states must be strengthened so that they can become partners in the process of creating economic coherence. When economies do not cohere, countries become breeding grounds for localized civil conflicts that often spill across national borders.

This book explains the necessary building blocks of economic coherence. It then develops a diagnostic approach to demonstrate how to identify impediments to the efficient functioning of essential economic processes. Finally, the book contains an extensive treatment of the policy-reform process, complete with a practical guide to how donors can work with governments to create economic coherence.

Daniel W. Bromley is Anderson-Bascom Professor (Emeritus) of applied economics at the University of Wisconsin-Madison, and Visiting Professor, Humboldt University-Berlin.

Glen D. Anderson is Senior Manager at International Resources Group, Washington, D.C.

Routledge Priorities for Development Economics
Edited by Paul Mosley, University of Sheffield, UK

VULNERABLE PEOPLE, VULNERABLE STATES

Redefining the development challenge

Daniel W. Bromley
and Glen D. Anderson

LONDON AND NEW YORK

First published 2012
by Routledge
2 Park Square, Milton Park, Abingdon, Oxon OX14 4RN

Simultaneously published in the USA and Canada
by Routledge
711 Third Avenue, New York, NY 10017

Routledge is an imprint of the Taylor & Francis Group, an informa business

British Library Cataloguing in Publication Data
A catalogue record for this book is available from the British Library

Library of Congress Cataloging in Publication Data
   Vulnerable people, vulnerable states: redefining the development
   challenge / Daniel W. Bromley and Glen D. Anderson.
      p. cm.
   1. Developing countries—Economic conditions. 2. Developing
   countries—Economic policy. 3. Developing countries—Politics and
   government. 4. Economic development I. Anderson, Glen D.
   (Glen Douglass), 1951- II. Title.
   HC59.7.B6888 2012
   338.9009172'4—dc23   2011051034

ISBN: 978-0-415-53451-2 (hbk)
ISBN: 978-0-415-53454-3 (pbk)
ISBN: 978-0-203-11332-5 (ebk)

Typeset in Bembo
by Cenveo Publisher Services

Printed and bound in Great Britain by
TJ International Ltd, Padstow, Cornwall

We dedicate this to Joyce and Marian for suffering our many long absences, but especially for their shared commitment to helping vulnerable people and vulnerable states.

CONTENTS

ILLUSTRATIONS

Figures

Tables

PREFACE

It has been approximately six decades since the *idea* of development worked its way into economics, international politics, and the public mind. As we explore here, this idea has undergone frequent revision as the practical problems, the conceptual understanding, and the needs of the developing countries have evolved. Our approach to this historic endeavor is respectful of this continual evolutionary process.

But our purpose here is to suggest that, in many respects, the traditional "discourse of development" has now run its course. We will suggest that the standard development catechism has not served poor people and poor countries very well. Nor has this approach always offered those from the outside a clear and meaningful picture of the unique settings and circumstances of disparate peoples and their manifold challenges. These flaws are both linguistic and perceptual. After all, the word "development" suggests a process with a rather known and desirable end state in mind. There are "developed" countries, and then there are the others—"underdeveloped" or, if one wishes to sound optimistic, "developing." It is taken for granted in the discourse of development that the latter countries will—and should—become more like the former countries. Indeed, the international development community is devoted to the task of implementing this convergence. It is said that the international development community is *fighting poverty*—and in so doing it is contributing to this historic quest for convergence. One prominent author casts this quest in terms of a "burden" to be shouldered by the developed world (Easterly 2006).

We seek here to move the conversation away from "development" and "fighting poverty." Instead, it is time to redefine the development challenge as one addressing the manifold problems of vulnerable people and vulnerable states. It is our view that the essential problem in the poorer countries of the world is *not* that they are not "developed." The pressing problem is, instead, that the millions of individuals living in those parts of the world are exposed—on a daily basis—to the unwelcome vicissitudes of bad economic and social outcomes. Some of those bad outcomes are the result of flawed government policies. Others are the result of drought, hurricanes, earthquakes, crop failures, floods, epidemics, and a changing climate. If those of us in the industrialized world are really serious about improving the life prospects of the 1.4 billion individuals scattered across the smaller latitudes, then attention must be paid to the persistent vulnerabilities of both individuals and nation-states.

We offer here the proposition that focusing development assistance on vulnerable people and vulnerable states opens the way to innovative strategies for helping the less fortunate individuals in the less promising settings and circumstances around the world.

ACKNOWLEDGMENTS

We wish to express our immense gratitude to Dr. Kenneth Baum in the United States Agency for International Development's Bureau for Economic Growth, Agriculture, and Trade for his belief in and unwavering support for the preparation of this book. He encouraged us to strike out in unconventional directions, and he provided invaluable comments on several earlier drafts of the manuscript. We also wish to thank Glen's colleagues at International Resources Group—Douglas Clark and Dr. James Tarrant, and former colleague Dr. Charles Benjamin, now President of the Near East Foundation—for their feedback and suggestions for improving the manuscript. Finally, several anonymous reviewers provided critical yet constructive comments on earlier versions of the manuscript.

FOREWORD

In the opening chapter of their new book, Daniel Bromley and Glen Anderson use the story of a Ghanaian farmer to vividly remind us that when the poor try to make a living, they face an insurmountable avalanche of barriers and costs. It is expensive being poor! And it makes them vulnerable. The reasons for their vulnerability? The rules that govern their economic lives are dysfunctional and incoherent. And because the poor cannot influence these many incoherent economic institutions, they become vulnerable.

To reduce vulnerability, the authors argue, we need to diagnose and repair the incoherence of the economic institutions that create the vulnerability. Creating economic coherence is, in the authors' view, a new and better development paradigm than the current one of fighting poverty through economic convergence, or removing binding constraints to growth. True, the authors concede, vulnerability has many aspects, and is difficult to measure. But better measurement of outcomes is not what will make a difference to the lives of those who are chronically vulnerable. Take the Millennium Development Goals. Because these focus on symptoms of, rather than reasons for, vulnerability, they do not provide the basis for a clear and practical strategy. Focusing on vulnerability and coherence, by contrast, holds the promise of giving us clarity of purpose and forcing us to think about causality and connections.

How to create more vulnerability-reducing coherence in an economy? Foster the enabling environment for markets to do their job, so that individuals can act, and transact, based on good information. Be clear about priorities and sequencing. Create the political space for innovation and adaptation, etc. This book is not just about rethinking old concepts and suggesting powerful new ones. It is also a practical guide. Highly recommended!

Rogier van den Brink, World Bank, USA

1
FROM CONVERGENCE TO COHERENCE

The new development opportunity

> More than one billion people—one sixth of the world's population—suffer from chronic hunger. Without enough food, adults struggle to work and children struggle to learn. Global food supplies must increase by an estimated 50 percent to meet expected demand in the next 20 years. Advancing sustainable agricultural-led growth increases the availability of food, keeps food affordable, and raises the incomes of the poor.
>
> (U.S. State Department)[1]

On being vulnerable

Imagine a Ghanaian farmer—we shall call him Kweku Owiredu—situated 100 kilometers from the major commercial center of Kumasi. He must acquire the bulk of his necessary agricultural inputs in Kumasi, and this is the only market for the wonderful restaurant-grade vegetables he produces and hopes to sell. Unfortunately, his farm is a "world away" from the bustle of Kumasi. The road over this modest stretch is often in bad condition—particularly during the rainy season. In addition, he can count on being stopped along the route two or three times by police looking for unlicenced vehicles and drivers, by highway officials looking for overweight trucks, and by forestry officials checking for evidence of illegal logging. Each stop may take as little as three to five minutes, but it can also take 30–45 minutes depending on traffic and the "mood" of those doing the checking. Kweku Owiredu will be required to offer a variety of exactions at each stop depending on the time of day (exactions are higher at night), what he is hauling, and other factors over which he has no control. His vegetables suffer in the heat and it is not unusual that 25 percent of his harvest will be damaged by the time he manages to arrive in Kumasi. It requires little imagination to understand that this story applies to virtually all transport corridors in sub-Saharan Africa—as well as in many developing countries (Bromley and Foltz 2011; Shleifer and Vishny 1993; Olken and Barron 2009).

But "highway robbery" is not the only impediment facing our farmer. Other aspects of his daily existence bear the marks of political and economic incoherence. He has never seen an agricultural extension agent, the electricity that allows him to pump irrigation water fails much too often, the surface irrigation system on which he must depend (when electricity is not available) is silted in and largely dysfunctional, fertilizer that he has ordered rarely arrives when needed—and when it does appear he can rarely afford it. He is unable to obtain production credit at any rate of interest, and his pest-control program is non-existent. Yields suffer. A nearby cement factory deposits limestone dust for many kilometers in all directions, and when the wind is from the South his tomatoes develop spots—rendering them unsuitable for the Kumasi market. The harvest is slow and uncertain. Spoilage haunts him.

At the end of the year, when he adds up his costs and revenues, it cannot be doubted that he wonders what might have been. What if most everything "worked well"? Just think what his net income might be if only the many incoherencies that plague his farming operation might somehow be eliminated.

At first glance this may appear to be just an "economic" problem. It is, however, a matter of debilitating incoherence in the constellation of institutional and organizational arrangements that define the domain of feasible action for the farmer. It is also a problem of governance because Kweku Owiredu has no possible means whereby he might eliminate the delays and bribes along the highway, he has no way to improve the reliability of electricity, he cannot influence the reliability of the supply network that cannot seem to deliver his much-needed fertilizer on time, nor does he stand any chance at all of bringing an agricultural extension agent to his neighborhood. He cannot have any effect on the dysfunctional surface irrigation system, on pollution from the cement factory, or on the flawed credit system. The economic system does not work because the political system does not work. More seriously, he is powerless to induce anything at all to work for him. The effects bearing down on him are *economic*—the reasons for his inability to change these debilitating effects are *political*. He is stuck with a whole constellation of incoherencies. These incoherencies sentence him to a life of unremitting hardship, of endless toil, of high hopes, and of higher impediments. Nothing works well, and there is nothing that he can do to alter that state of affairs. Kweku Owiredu personifies vulnerability.

Dysfunctional economies do not cohere. And the price of incoherence for individuals such as Kweku Owiredu is a life spent on the margin of survival. Improvement is not an option. Rectifying incoherence is about enhanced governance processes. It concerns *policy reform*. While it is common to think of the official (top-down) aspects of policy reform, we shall stress here that policy reform must also be understood to accommodate the opportunity for Kweku Owiredu to have an effect on the debilitating state of institutional incoherence. He requires opportunities to address his own vulnerabilities.

Our Ghanaian farmer is exposed to incoherencies, his livelihood prospects are profoundly undermined by the absence of necessary resilience, and he lacks the opportunity to rectify his miserable circumstances.[2]

We define vulnerability at the individual (family) level as a combination of chronic exposure, insufficient resilience, and an absence of options to overcome the persistent adversities that define daily life. At the national level, vulnerability is a collective inability to create and sustain the economic surplus—and the political capacity—necessary to overcome persistent buffeting of natural events, global economic shocks, and domestic turmoil precipitated by these shocks, or by chronic political disaffection.

Vulnerable states can be thought of as both the cause and the effect of vulnerable people. Some states are exposed to droughts, tsunamis, and earthquakes, while others are exposed to insurgents from within, or from neighboring countries. Some poor countries have a capacity for resilience—a deep treasury, effective infrastructure, a functioning militia, good communications—while the majority do not. And some states have the opportunity to seek help from neighbors, while most are situated in a neighborhood of similarly vulnerable states with no opportunity to be of assistance.

The reality of vulnerable people and vulnerable states is not a new phenomenon. Emphasizing the vexing challenge of international development through the lens of vulnerability is—however—a departure from the norm. And we believe that a focus on vulnerability provides the necessary clarity of purpose to seek alternatives to how international development assistance is both conceptualized and implemented.

A new opportunity

The global community is now faced with a promising opportunity. Over the next several years, those who work on the Millennium Development Goals (MDGs) will begin to confirm the large number of discouraging outcomes that are anticipated (and well understood) by those who labor on behalf of the world's poor. By the target date of 2015 very few countries in Africa will have made any progress with respect to those development goals (World Bank 2005a). Indeed it is possible that a few countries will have lost ground since the MDGs were launched (United Nations Development Programme 2007). This cannot be a surprise, and in what follows we make the case that exercises such as the MDGs are profoundly misguided.

Indeed, they border on the counter-productive. First, the goals and their associated indicators are lagging symptoms. That is, they are depictions of particular outcomes from the past and therefore are of little help in guiding development actions that will improve circumstances in the future. Obscured in programs that focus on symptoms is the necessary logic of seeking reasons for those results. If reasons are not the central diagnostic interest, development assistance efforts and funds are squandered. With "development fatigue" a constant threat, it will be tragic if this flawed approach leads to a lessened commitment to the problems of vulnerable people and vulnerable states. This means that careful attention must be paid to clear causal relationships that connect incentives and actions with current unwelcome outcomes—the observed symptoms that receive so much attention in the MDGs.

The second problem is that the existence of the MDGs becomes a rationale—an excuse—for the design and implementation of new development programs and projects that will focus on these symptoms rather than on the reasons for—and underlying causes of—the problems most in need of correction. Development assistance cannot succeed if it is chained to this flawed approach.

The escape from a focus on symptoms and contrived "development goals" is to make vulnerable people and vulnerable states the central units of analysis. Doing so reminds us that the overriding purpose of development assistance must be to create *economic coherence*. The most important question must always concern whether or not an economy coheres. With that in mind, the point of development assistance must be to make sure that any and all development assistance projects and programs effectively enhance the coherence of a national economy.

Economic coherence is not something that is created and then locked in place once and for all. An economy is always in the process of becoming. For some nations, and at particular times, that process of becoming will be constructive—the general structure and processes of the economy are improved upon. Jobs are created at a rate approximating the annual net addition of young people seeking employment. Technical innovation proceeds at a pace that renders a somewhat greater value of total output so that the incomes of those engaged in the economy will gradually rise. The quality of the human capital stock improves because the educational system gives rise to a renewable cohort of educated and well-trained individuals ready to assume a productive role in the economy. Notice that this evolving coherence does not just automatically happen. Economic coherence must be created—and it must be sustained.

New economic policies are the necessary means by which coherence is created. Policy reform must be understood as a continual process of *institutional refinement* through which economic coherence is sustained and enhanced. While much attention has been focused on environmentally sustainable development, too little attention has been paid to economically sustainable development. When development is economically sustainable then the burdens to befall vulnerable people are identified, diagnosed, and gradually meliorated. And when vulnerable people are rendered less vulnerable it follows that the political and economic vulnerability of nation-states will be gradually reduced.

As above, vulnerable states are the cause and the effect of vulnerable people—and vulnerable people are the cause and the effect of vulnerable states. The process of rectifying vulnerable people *and* vulnerable states is one of simultaneous imperatives and implications.

The key to creating economic coherence is that national policies must be continually assessed and refined in line with emerging exigencies and needs. These necessary changes will be driven by shifting relative prices, by new technical opportunities, by new external threats and opportunities, and by unexpected perturbations. British Prime Minister Harold Macmillan, on being asked the most challenging aspect of being a statesman, is reported to have said: "Events, my dear boy, events."

Coherent economies are dynamic because their policies are purposefully adaptive. Dynamic economies possess the necessary political structures and processes to address the problems of their most vulnerable people—and in doing so they ameliorate the economic and social pathologies that, if allowed to remain unattended and to fester, result in vulnerable states. Unfortunately, most seriously poor countries are on economic trajectories that might be described as *downwardly asymptotic*. These economies are asymptotic because they tend toward a low-level stasis from which escape is difficult, if not impossible. In downwardly asymptotic economies there is very little that individuals can do that will nudge the economy out of its malaise. The inevitable inertia becomes increasingly pervasive and self-fulfilling. As this situation persists, prospects for individual improvement remain elusive. Many agricultural households withdraw into subsistence production (autarky) in the face of dysfunctional markets for inputs and for their products. High costs of credit starve the economy of the necessary leverage to undertake promising new initiatives. The status quo becomes the norm. Any changes seem quite impossible to imagine, and justifiably so. Meaningful change is an infrequent visitor.

Much of the standard development agenda—motivated by the idea that the purpose of development is to fight poverty—proceeds from a presumption of an economy considered to be in need of a little better system of agricultural credit, or much less in the way of subsidies for staple foods, or fewer perverse subsidies for farmers, or much less corruption. In addition, there is thought to be a need for policies to encourage technical change, to introduce high-yielding crop varieties (perhaps genetically modified organisms), or to increase school attendance and retention, or to increase savings rates, or to improve the suite of macroeconomic policies so that the presumed dynamic processes might be refined.

The rest of the economy (and its processes) are generally assumed to be working well enough and so economic policy in the service of development is thought of as a process of fine-tuning an economy that is structurally sound but in need of some improved incentives at key points in the system. The general story is to "get prices right" and then the requisite dynamism will be attained (or restored). It is noted that those countries with "good" policies can put development assistance to effective use, while those countries with "bad" policies cannot benefit from development assistance (Burnside and Dollar 2000). The cynic might note that if countries have "good" policies they should not need development assistance. And if their policies are not "good" then no amount of development assistance will help. What then of development assistance?

It may be noticed that this is the logic—the approach—of the Millennium Challenge Corporation (MCC). Here, countries are "pre-qualified" to determine the extent to which they are on a trajectory to make good use of development assistance. Ironically, those countries that are the most vulnerable, and those countries with the most vulnerable people, cannot possibly qualify. Do they count?

The problem is apparent. As long as development assistance is driven by the quest for economic growth as a means to solve poverty, the entire activity is held hostage by that mysterious black box called "good policies" (or "bad policies"). To put the problem in causal terms, these policies—whether good or bad—comprise the transmission mechanism that must convert development assistance in its various forms into measurable evidence of economic growth and poverty reduction. Unfortunately, it is a transmission mechanism that defies robust and meaningful assessments of its instrumental properties. The standard development approach comes dangerously close to the unfortunate position that good policies bring about good outcomes, and bad policies do not. This ironic paradox of development assistance provides the very best evidence that it is time for a new approach.

The essential alternative must be one that cannot be defeated by "bad policies." That is, development assistance must be re-crafted in such a way that it is impossible for bad policies to stand between implementation of programmatic activities (the inputs) and their intended effects (desired outcomes).

An emphasis on the tangible problems of vulnerable people and vulnerable states gets right to the tasks for which development assistance was launched in the 1960s (Arndt 1987). If population growth continues unabated, if HIV/AIDS is ravaging a population, if economic policies cannot generate plausible jobs and livelihood prospects, if natural resources are degraded, and if the current mix of infrastructural goods and services—communication, education, highways, health care—is degraded and dysfunctional then prospects for escaping an asymptotic trajectory and its unwanted outcomes are not encouraging.

Our emphasis on vulnerable people and vulnerable states has nothing at all to do with humanitarian relief efforts in the wake of natural disasters. Those efforts are essential components of responding to crises when they strike poor (or rich) nations. But the development-assistance enterprise must come to be about chronic vulnerabilities, not acute events that demand a focused and coordinated response from the international community. Notice, however, the connection between natural disasters and chronic vulnerabilities. Acute events such as earthquakes or typhoons are rendered more problematic precisely because vulnerable states are mired in chronic incoherence. Such states lack the means to reduce exposure to these unwelcome events, these states are unable to mobilize the necessary resources to bolster resilience, and such states are bereft of the organizational capacity and financial means to prepare for the next such event. And so they reel in the face of repeated shocks.

A consistent focus on economic coherence reinforces the point that development assistance must now be reconstituted to become *an activity whose primary purpose is to diagnose and mitigate the pernicious vulnerabilities of individuals and families in downwardly asymptotic economies*. This new approach holds promise that economies stuck on seriously asymptotic trajectories can be transformed and nudged onto dynamic trajectories.

This new approach to development is justified by a realization that the pressing challenges of social and economic development—as conceived and carried out over the past half-century—are no longer suited to the circumstances facing the world in the early decades of a new century. Recall that the animating idea of development over the past decades has been *convergence*—that with financial and technical assistance from the relatively developed nations of the industrialized North, those countries in the agrarian South would gradually achieve economic and social "development." These achievements would, of course, require good governance, but it is here that the international community could show the way by good example. Democracy would be introduced and nurtured.

Sadly, the history of development assistance programs has a seen a long list of promising initiatives go in and out of fashion—import substitution, infant-industries, appropriate technology, structural adjustment, micro-finance, sustainable development, the Washington Consensus, eliminating corruption, fighting poverty, and now the Millennium Development Goals. Throughout this period of thematic fixes and visions, the hope and expectation has always been that the remaining poor countries would achieve "economic growth and development." In other words, the persistent divisions of rich and poor, industrial and agrarian, North and South would eventually disappear under the programmatic initiatives of the international community. *Economic convergence* would overtake the long-standing disparities in social and economic conditions. Despite the very best efforts, and billions of dollars of foreign assistance, over 50 years of concerted and quite aggressive development assistance has failed to produce economic convergence (Pritchett 1997).

With this disappointing record in hand, it is necessary to reassess long-held notions concerning the purposes of development assistance. It is our contention that the traditional emphasis on *economic convergence* must now be replaced by an emphasis on *economic coherence*. This new focus on economic coherence underwrites a programmatic commitment to the manifold fragilities of vulnerable people and vulnerable states.

We believe there are compelling moral arguments to be made on behalf of an emphasis on addressing individual and household vulnerabilities. We believe that many international political problems can be better understood, and more easily meliorated, if the focus of international development assistance can be shifted away from stimulating GDP growth and "fighting poverty." Development assistance must now be refocused on the vexing problems and challenges facing vulnerable people and vulnerable states.

For the most part, the current preoccupation with convergence makes little allowance for countries that are hit by periodic natural disasters such as hurricanes, torrential rains, or drought. Of course it is noted that the Philippines, Indonesia, and parts of the Caribbean are frequently inundated by violent tropical storms. But the full developmental implication of such natural disasters is not adequately incorporated into the standard program of "fighting poverty."

More seriously, as we show below, the idea of convergence makes no allowance for nation-states in much of Africa and the Middle East that have minimally comprehensive governance. Vast areas of meager economic potential in much of this semi-arid region have not been understood in terms of the absence of a coherent state that could reach into those desolate corners and provide services in exchange for taxes and the other obligations of citizenship. The colonial history of Africa, whose overriding purpose was aggressive extraction of both people (slaves) and particular natural resources (timber, ivory, minerals), holds important implications for how the idea of development ought to be conceived and implemented on that continent. Little of this seems to get noticed in the quest for convergence.

A focus on vulnerability, on the other hand, starts from the premise that the underlying causal structures and processes of downwardly asymptotic economies are not coherent—that is the reason why those economies are on such bad trajectories. People and nations are vulnerable precisely because the economy is not set up to be responsive and adaptive. In many settings, post-colonial governments have continued the extraction of economic surplus, with the only difference being that the economic rents now accrue to indigenous leaders and their ravenous coterie rather than to the colonial economies of Europe. The ironic expression of this problem is "Same car, different driver."

The most effective way to rescue asymptotic economies and their citizens from vulnerability is to make sure that these economies are characterized by governance structures—and economic policies—that are quick to recognize problematic situations, and that have the capacity and ability to adapt to urgent threats. Vulnerability is mitigated if governments are responsive and adaptable to current—and new—problematic situations.

Implications

The historic motive for development assistance—to bring about convergence between the industrial North and the agrarian South—is no longer tenable. With the deadline for achieving the Millennium Development Goals nearly upon us (2015), it cannot be claimed that many of the very poorest countries will be able to show any substantial progress. The reasons are apparent. There is no strategic vision, and there is no causal structure. The MDGs represent a catalogue of negotiated symptoms that are somehow to be rectified. More seriously, there is no recognition that achieving certain politically negotiated targets by 2015 is very different indeed from creating sustainable economic trajectories that assure economic coherence into the foreseeable future. What happens in 2016 and beyond?

If failure is indeed the result, it implies that many years and billions of dollars of foreign development assistance will have come to naught. It is too easy blame the countries in which this lavish activity and financial assistance have been concentrated. There is no attention paid to whether the logic and approach of development assistance is itself flawed. Recent assessments hold little that is both innovative and promising (Collier 2007; Easterly 2001, 2006; Sachs 2005, 2008; World Bank 2005b).

Our contention here is that the time is right for shifting development assistance away from fighting poverty. If the international development community is to succeed, it is necessary that attention be redirected toward those problems that plague vulnerable people. This new focus will necessarily concern the incoherent institutional foundations of social and economic relations. Correcting those incoherencies will begin to address the multiple problems of vulnerable people and vulnerable states.

2

ON ECONOMIC COHERENCE

The concept of economic coherence

Our primary commitment here is to a development-assistance agenda that will help
to overcome the plight of vulnerable people and vulnerable states. These dual vulnerabilities are important symptoms of flaws in the way that national economies are
structured, and in how they function. If the persistence of vulnerable people and
vulnerable states is to be rectified, these structural and functional deficiencies must
be eliminated. The pressing challenge confronting development assistance is to help
economies to cohere. Consider Figure 2.1.

Here we depict economies as consisting of four essential components. On the far
left we see: (1) the current set of endowments (personal wealth, the stock of physical
capital); (2) the existing quantity and quality of natural resources; and (3) the stock
(and quality) of available technology. These aspects set the stage for subsequent economic activity—we refer to this component as the *Data* of the economy. The idea
of "data" suggests that these attributes are given and cannot be changed in the short
run. Here we find the factors and circumstances that both enable economic processes and that help to impel those processes forward. If a nation's citizens have scant
personal wealth (no savings), if there are few natural resources, and if the stock of

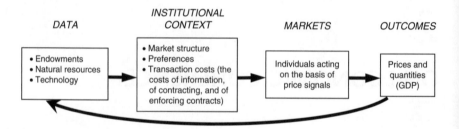

FIGURE 2.1 Coherent economic processes

technology is limited and of doubtful efficacy, there cannot be much hope for individual prosperity and economic growth.

The process of moving forward is then mediated by the next component—the *Institutional Context*. Here we encounter: (1) market structure (Are markets competitive or monopolized?); (2) consumer preferences; and (3) several varieties of transactions costs: (a) the costs of gaining information about market opportunities; (b) the costs of negotiating contracts so that those opportunities might be realized; and (c) the costs of enforcing those contracts once they have been completed. The *Institutional Context* determines how the economy's *Data* can be deployed in households and firms as individuals go about their daily lives as farmers, employees, managers, owners, and consumers interacting through existing market processes.

Notice that the *Institutional Context* comprises the important pre-market settings and circumstances that mediate between the *Data* of the economy and how *Markets* will function in that economy. To put it another way, the specifics of market structure, of consumer preferences, and of the three categories of transaction costs constitute the institutional "filter" that pre-figures which market opportunities will be pursued, what the probable payoffs will be for those activities, and which market opportunities will be precluded. If market structure and performance comprise impediments to particular economic activities, or if high transaction costs prevent market activity, low-grade autarky will be the inevitable result (Bromley 2008a; Bromley and Chavas 1989). Autarky destroys the prospects for economic progress of individuals and therefore of states.

On the other hand, if the *Institutional Context* is conducive to efficient market processes then the economy will consist of a constellation of prices and quantities (*Outcomes*) that will result in the maximum possible level of national income (GDP) over a specific period of time. If those conditions can be sustained, the economy will continue to offer promising income opportunities and will thereby achieve gradual growth in GDP.

We see in Figure 2.1 that there are two general sources of poor economic performance that will give rise to vulnerable people and vulnerable states. The first source of deficient economic outcomes can be traced to deficient **Data**. The nation may suffer from a lack of natural resources (e.g. Haiti, Somalia), it may have limited technological capacity, or there could be little savings to fuel needed investment.

COHERENCE: A PRACTICAL GUIDE

The idea *of economic coherence* may be elusive. But coherence is easily grasped, and then it can be transported into the realm of a national economy.

Imagine a well-disciplined soccer team—each player has particular skills and therefore is an essential part of the overall success of the team. As the ball is advanced down the pitch, the separate parts of the collection of individuals must be in the right position, and each must be prepared to carry out quite specific roles when called upon. The successful teams demonstrate a high degree of coherence. They work well as a unit.

Economic coherence shares the same attributes—the parts of the economy have specific roles to play, and when called upon they play those roles as expected.

Often all three conditions will be present. The second source of inadequate economic outcomes is found in the **Institutional context**. It is here that development assistance, especially policy reform, is necessary.

From the depiction in Figure 2.1 we see that the sole purpose of a market economy is to generate information that will be useful in guiding individual action concerning allocation of scarce resources—that is what markets are for. That is what market economies do—they produce information about promising prospects. There is no central planner dictating production and consumption "targets." Notice that the arrows in Figure 2.1 depict information flows from one phase to the next. When that information is contentful—meaning that the information contains very little "noise"—then the allocative decisions based on that information will be economically rational. In general terms, economically rational allocations mean that it is impossible to change those allocations without reducing the aggregate monetary value of a nation's output (GDP). The economy is on the "Pareto frontier." On the other hand, when noise distorts or blocks out pertinent market information, resource allocation will be flawed and the resulting level of GDP will be diminished. From such circumstances, personal as well as national vulnerability easily sets in.

We see that markets are information-generating systems. The information generated by markets is the result (the effect) of prior choices by producers and consumers. This same information then provides important reasons for current and future choices by producers and consumers. The arrows between the four components of a market economy are suggestive of the flow of information from left to right in Figure 2.1. Information about endowments, resources, and technology "enters into" the *Institutional Context* and is there "processed" by consumer preferences, by the structure of various markets, and by the nature of transaction costs. When that information leaves the *Institutional Context*, and is acted upon by individuals, it provides useful and valuable reasons for particular actions by consumers and producers as they engage in market activities.

Economies are coherent when the information content of market signals leads to efficient allocative decisions. But what are these "signals" of such importance to economic performance? An important signal received by a consumer would concern the price for a given quantity and quality of a certain product. If this individual purchases the product at that price then this price and quantity information becomes an important signal that this particular product—of this quality—is "worth" what the individual paid for it. Or consider an entrepreneur who assesses a particular piece of land with the intention to invest in it so as to produce some commodity. The quality of that land is a signal to the individual concerning its productive potential. If the entrepreneur decides to purchase that land, its price is a signal to others of the value of the land. If the farmer must acquire a loan to purchase the land then the quality of that land (*Data*) and the economic prospects (*Institutional Context*), as well as the credit history of the individual, comprise important signals to potential creditors.

When the entrepreneur successfully uses the land and other inputs to produce some commodity, the farmer's asking price in the market is a signal concerning the costs of production and a hoped-for return for his labor time and management skills. The eventual sale price represents a signal that will help others to form expectations about the worth of what is being produced on that land—and hence of the market value of the land so engaged. We see that a market economy is a signaling mechanism—all participants act on signals, and in acting they in turn generate yet new signals that are useful to others as they contemplate particular actions.

ECONOMIC NOISE

The idea of *noise* in economic information refers to the absence of reliable and credible information about economic possibilities. For instance, a grain buyer moving through rural Kenya may makes offers to farmers that differ radically from village to village. There is no economic basis for those different offers aside from quality differences, and the varying costs of moving the grain to a central market. The buyer's price information is too "noisy" to be a reliable signal to farmers concerning the true market value of their grain. When farmers communicate among themselves, they find this price spread anomalous and it raises suspicion among sellers.

These signals are flows of information. Good signals are clear and this allows them to be easily understood. These clear signals contain useful—valuable—information. On the other hand, bad signals are weak and are accompanied by a great deal of "noise." Such signals are unclear and difficult to decipher. In such cases, the information content of these signals is low. There is little information in such signals because it is most difficult to be sure about what is being observed—"noise" obscures important information.

Figure 2.1 shows an economy that works well—it coheres because the flow of information through that economy is contentful. However, economies with defective signals about promising prospects do not cohere, and they will therefore abound with vulnerable people. When these circumstances persist, such countries become vulnerable states. That is, if the economy does not cohere, individuals will be thwarted in their efforts to improve their lives. As with Kweku the Ghanaian farmer, every turn is blocked—either by flawed signals from the *Institutional Context*, or by political problems that prevent the flawed economic signals from being corrected. A well-functioning market economy is the result of: (1) a persistent and ongoing process of legal arrangements and decrees emanating from parliaments and the courts; (2) administrative rulings that add specificity to parliamentary laws and legal decrees; and (3) a commitment from the political community that these legal arrangements (laws, decrees, and rules) will be useless in the absence of a widespread ethical commitment to compliance—backed up by honest enforcement when necessary.

While we have focused attention on the many economic and political incapacities of a single individual—Kweku Owiredu—there are millions of individuals in a similar situation. Indeed, in a recent report from the United Nations Development Programme we see evidence of the persistent scope of persistent vulnerabilities. The authors note:

> The main objective of this study is to compute an international poverty threshold based on the food requirement to ensure an adequate calorie intake for the world's poorest. The study proposes a new methodology based on consumer theory to provide a caloric based international poverty threshold. Using this methodology, the international poverty line is estimated to be equal to $1.22 in 1993 PPP exchange rates. According to this new yardstick, almost 1.37 billion people were poor around the world in 2001. The study also provides global estimates of hunger, according to which 13.28 percent of the world population—equivalent to 687 million people—suffered from hunger in 2001.
>
> *(Kakwani and Son 2006: 1)*

The aggregate implication of this vulnerability—borne of economic incapacity— means that national economies gradually slide into a state of low-grade disarray from which escape is virtually impossible. We depict this situation in Figure 2.2.

Here, the information content in the economy is neither robust nor contentful. The necessary transmission of good information from the *Data*, mediated by the *Institutional Context*, then acted upon by individuals in the *Market,* yields a constellation of goods and services (*Prices and Quantities*) that is inferior to what would be

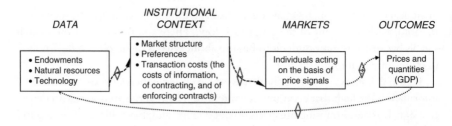

FIGURE 2.2 Economic processes showing incoherence

possible if the economy cohered. This situation is depicted in Figure 2.2 by the crooked and dubious connectors (arrows) that suggest the degraded quality of market information as the process moves forward. In practical terms, by the time individuals can interact in markets, the quality of the signals (information) upon which rational action can be based is so poor that all potential economic gains will have been dissipated—either because of imperfect market processes or inordinately high transaction costs.

While the foregoing discussion concerns the institutional aspects of a market economy, the physical infrastructure is also essential to economic coherence. That is, market economies require both institutional and physical infrastructures if they are to cohere. We refer to both the institutional and physical aspects as the transactions infrastructures of an economy.

The physical infrastructure provides the logistical means whereby goods and services, including labor, can move in response to the signals flowing through the economy. Physical infrastructure is essential to economic coherence because market participants cannot credibly commit to market transactions if there are no means whereby the goods that have been bought and sold can be moved from seller to buyer. As with Kweku Owiredu, roads are often impassible during the rainy season. Even when dry they are rough and impede travel.

These aspects are found in the *Data* component of Figures 2.1 and 2.2. That is, the transportation network comprises an important aspect of a country's techno-logical capacity. In addition to the road network, the quantity and quality of a nation's trucking fleet and railroad system is an important dimension of the techno-logical infrastructure available to the economy.

In Figure 2.3 we depict a slightly different representation of an economy. Here we see a major urban center linked to the world economy, there is a major market center linking the agricultural economy to the urban center, and there is the rural economy where the majority of individuals reside. Households sell labor to firms and receive wages/salaries in return. This income is then spent in firms in exchange for goods and services flowing to households. Farm households are integrated with the agricultural enterprise. The rural economy in such countries generally has a

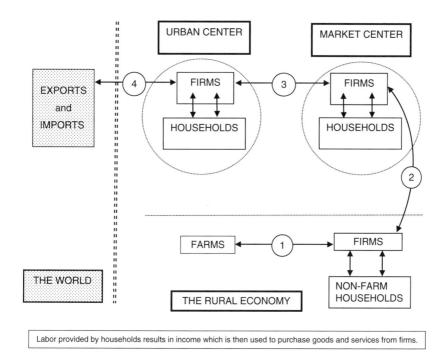

FIGURE 2.3 Graphical depiction of transaction infrastructures

small non-farm component that is the first (and possibly only) link to the rest of the national economy. Arrows depict the reciprocal movement of commodities and services in exchange for money.

Figure 2.3 helps to illustrate a fundamental idea concerning coherence in a market economy. As above, the importance of signals in a market is matched by the importance of the physical infrastructure along which goods and services must move. Initiatives concerned with improving market infrastructures of developing economies would necessarily start with a diagnostic commitment to discern those impediments that now preclude the coherent operation of market processes.[1] This effort would be concerned to identify physical barriers (faulty roads, dysfunctional road networks, flawed communications systems, etc.) as well as institutional barriers (corruption, credit-rationing, faulty pricing arrangements, theft).

The primary purpose of development assistance focused on creating economic coherence would be to help economic processes—the meaningful flows of information and goods—function in a manner that encourages productive activity rather than grudging resignation and withdrawal into autarky. If that is successful, enhanced agricultural production, food security, and general economic development will be the result. We offer brief comments on each of the four commodity corridors shown in Figure 2.3.

Corridor #1

This corridor is the basic connector for farmers and those rural firms which provide farmers with necessary inputs, and which are usually the first handler for many agricultural products. Examples of market signals and physical inputs that must move through the transactions infrastructure in order to enhance production and marketing are: (1) credit markets offering production credit at feasible prices; (2) reliable price information—and market prospects—for inputs: (3) assured availability of all essential inputs (fertilizer, seed, herbicides and pesticides, technical assistance); and (4) reliable and efficient irrigation systems—including electricity for pumps—to make sure that necessary water is available when needed.

The market for agricultural products must also function well along this corridor. As before, there must be: (1) reliable price information—and market opportunities—for all agricultural output; (2) hedging opportunities for farmers to moderate exposure to price uncertainty; and (3) corruption-free movement of goods along road networks throughout the rural economy. Reflecting back on the problems of Kweku Owiredu, it is along this corridor that most of his problems arise.

Corridor #2

This corridor connects rural input and product firms with their suppliers and buyers in the major market town. Economic coherence along this corridor requires: (1) corruption-free movement of goods in both directions; (2) reliable price information; (3) legal arrangements to reduce the risk in moving large quantities of products; and (4) reliable and good-quality transportation system—roads, rail, trucks, storage and forwarding facilities.

With reference to Figure 2.1, the institutional context will have a great influence on the manner in which the necessary economic processes can function along this corridor.

Corridor #3

This corridor connects firms in the major market town with counterpart firms in the urban center. As with corridor #2, here there must be: (1) corruption-free movement of goods in both directions; and (2) legal conditions to protect the movement of products and agricultural inputs.

Corridor #4

This corridor is the country's connection to the global economy. If particular aspects of local agricultural production are to move into world markets, and if necessary inputs from abroad are to arrive in a timely fashion, this corridor must offer: (1) reliable information about world prices; (2) quick and comprehensive processing of all international certification protocols, and (3) corruption-free port (air and sea) processing and logistics.

Economic coherence in practice

The conceptual approach to creating coherence can now be related to the programs and projects of the various development assistance agencies. If such activities are to succeed in creating economic coherence, two conditions are required: (1) development assistance agencies must recognize the legitimacy of a competent sovereign (a responsive government) as an essential collaborator in this new development approach; and (2) development assistance programs must focus attention on institutional change—policy reform—to enhance the scope and content of productive individual behaviors. Economic incoherence is parasitic on individual initiative. This necessarily implies that development assistance programs must move away from the current abundance of nice-sounding initiatives—food security, empowerment, sustainable development—and turn their attention to those efforts that will make national economies work as they must if the problems of vulnerable people are to be overcome. Doing so will also reduce the extent to which vulnerable states become mired in dysfunction. Economic coherence is the *sine qua non* for these desired transformations.

If there is to be improvement in the life prospects of several billion vulnerable people in the world, that desired result will only come through programs to strengthen governments and their capacity for governance. And the central dimension of this need to strengthen governments and governance is concerned with policy reform. That thematic work would have two broad purposes: (1) creating an enabling environment for gradual economic progress; and (2) creating an adaptive economy.

An enabling environment

The first task for any government is to create an enabling and reasonably predictable economic environment within which individuals can form plausible expectations about the possible payoffs from various commercial and industrial initiatives. This is the information component of markets discussed in conjunction with Figures 2.1 and 2.2. When these expectations are absent, individual initiative is stifled. In the face of repeated failure to realize gains, most individuals eventually become resigned to an existence of minimal expectations and minimal rewards. Individuals slip into a pattern of habituated behavior and the economy suffers accordingly. Vulnerability spreads.

The centrality of policy reform is found in the need for governments to implement an enduring strategy that accomplishes three purposes: (1) creating a well-functioning national market; (2) enhancing that national market as it continues to evolve; and (3) supporting that national market over time as new problems arise.

The creation of a national market entails the establishment of the necessary legal underpinnings—the institutional conditions—of production and exchange.[2] When governments enhance markets they nurture and facilitate the evolution of production and exchange activities so that transaction costs remain low, so that credit markets evolve and rectify liquidity problems, so that factor and product markets emerge and improve in concert with the growth in production, and so that the expansion of the market through inter-regional (and international) trade becomes feasible. When governments support markets, they acknowledge the more mature (hands-off) role of governments to step back and make sure that the evolving economic system continues to function in the interest of its participants— farmers, shopkeepers, small manufacturers, traders, import and export firms, agricultural product and supply firms, and other economic entities.

National governments must establish an institutional structure that will encourage productive initiatives on the part of individuals, and they must create the means and opportunities for that institutional structure (that legal architecture) to be modified through time as social and economic conditions warrant. There is both a static and a dynamic dimension to creating economic coherence.

The static part concerns the need to have an institutional structure that provides security of expectations without removing the necessary risk that keeps entrepreneurs alert and agile. The dynamic part concerns the need for continual adjustment in the institutional architecture—the legal foundations of the economy—to make sure that the economy remains attuned to new opportunities and new challenges. Yet this dynamism must not create so much uncertainty that reasonable expectations are difficult to form. The delicate balance requires predictability without rigidity, and flexibility without randomness. The purpose of policy reform is to create these conditions and imperatives.

Of course different countries have different institutional arrangements and thus individuals in those countries will have different fields of action open to them. Control over land in different societies is a reflection of differing historical patterns of interaction that show up as different institutional arrangements over grazing land, access to water, and other important economic activities. What is the nature of property relations with respect to agricultural land? Who can and who cannot harvest trees from particular plots of land? Who—if anyone—may dump industrial wastes into lakes and rivers? If dumping is possible, can it be done for free, or are there fees associated with those discharges? Are workers financially protected against accidents in the workplace? Are there wage and work-condition agreements that protect workers? May workers strike over those wages and work conditions? Are local schools open to all children? Must families pay school fees to send their children to school? May girls also attend those schools? What fiscal arrangements exist for the construction and maintenance of schools? How are teachers' salaries financed? Is there a maximum age for girls in such schools? Is dowry or bride-price prevalent or is it outlawed? Who is responsible for agricultural extension services? Who are the primary beneficiaries of such services? Must farmers pay for extension services? If so, how much, and how are those fees levied? How is water allocated on irrigation systems? Do those at the head-end of such systems receive favorable allocations?

What is the structure and organization of agricultural credit markets in rural areas? How is the rural credit system organized and regulated? Are there two distinct agricultural credit systems—one for purchasing land and another for seasonal pro-duction credit? Are agricultural leases and tenancy arrangements under the control of politically powerful landlords? Do labor markets exist (and function reasonably well) in rural areas? Is child labor prevalent? What is the structure of agricultural input and product markets—are they reasonably competitive or are those markets characterized by economic concentration? Which agricultural inputs are subsidized by the state? What incentives exist for land consolidation? Are there upper limits on farm size? Does primogeniture or partible inheritance define the bequeathing of agricultural land to offspring? Can rural residents receive particular health services? Are rural women discriminated against in particular roles? Are legal-aid clinics present for the poor and disadvantaged? Is the judicial system impartial? Are judges appointed or elected? Are contracts equitably enforced? Are debtors and creditors protected by efficient and incentive-compatible bankruptcy law? Are farmers rewarded for land-use decisions that contribute to biodiversity conservation?

Each of these examples constitutes the economic institutions that matter for economic coherence and thus the vulnerability of individuals and of nation-states.

An adaptive economy

An economy is always in the process of becoming. An adaptive economy requires that public policy be approached with clear phases (stages) in mind. First, inevitable scarcities suggest the need to concentrate financial and managerial resources in the most promising growth centers. Second, this need follows from the requirement to gain a clear understanding of the particularistic growth and development opportu-nities in a specific (and defined) set of geographic locations. Finally, meaningful development policy must formulate plausible scenarios of evolution in the special-ized economy of each particular location. Doing so avoids the seemingly random and scattered approaches we see in many development programs. Bringing eco-nomic coherence requires knowing what to do, and knowing in what particular order it must be done. Not all problems are urgent. The key to creating economic coherence is being clear about the order in which the necessary actions must be introduced and implemented.

Development initiatives will be successful when promising prospects are located in various regions, when local political and economic leaders are engaged in the process of identifying the most promising development prospects (projects and pro-grams), when donor assistance is creative in articulating how the central govern-ment can play a limited but necessary catalytic role in each of these settings and programs, and when long-term evolutionary trajectories are launched that seem likely to produce the desired results. This sequenced approach allows for the devel-opment of a meaningful strategy with clear indications concerning when—and under what conditions—the central government can withdraw from its early cata-lytic role and devolve the enhancement and support functions to local governments, local political processes, and local economic initiative. The expectation is that this phased approach will evolve and gradually induce increased economic activity in ever-larger zones around the original project-specific nodes. This approach will generally result in a multiplier effect that can then become the stimulus for yet greater economic activity spreading out from these specific nodes.

Local political leaders can be important entrepreneurs in this regard. Indeed, the dramatic success of China's economic transformation along the southeast coast can be attributed to a process of empowering provincial governors, county officials, mayors, and other political leaders to create a political and economic climate that will attract new investment and new entrepreneurial activity. This process is enhanced to the extent that such leaders compete among themselves to attract new economic activity (Bromley and Yao 2006). The central government must play a role here so that each region—a large state/province or perhaps several smaller states/provinces—can benefit somewhat proportionately from this effort to stimulate new economic activity. In some instances the NGO sector might be mobilized to play a role in this effort to induce economic development.

A few brief comments on "fighting poverty"

The World Bank is a vital source of financial and technical assistance to developing countries around the world:

> Our mission is to fight poverty with passion and professionalism for lasting results and to help people help themselves and their environment by providing resources, sharing knowledge, building capacity and forging partnerships in the public and private sectors.[3]

The idea of poverty—and the "fight" against it— dominates the prevailing development discourse. The literature is suffused with studies on poverty, there is a large though dubious literature on "poverty traps," and international donors such as the World Bank claim that their *raison d'être* is straightforward—they are "fighting poverty." There are now many measures of the nature and extent of poverty. Sometimes it will be rendered as the number of people living on less than some amount per day—usually $1.00 or $2.00 (perhaps now, with inflation, $1.25 and $2.25). There is relative poverty and there is absolute poverty. There are measures of the depth of poverty, and there are other indicators that will be used to make the point. Indeed, in 2008, when cereal prices in the developing world increased, it was said that even more families "slipped into poverty." It seems that there is income poverty, expenditure poverty, and asset poverty (Carter and Barrett 2006). There are poverty traps and "fractal" poverty traps (Azariadis 1996; Barrett and Swallow 2006).

It seems that the "idea of poverty" is an all-purpose notion that is useful in highlighting the fate of millions of desperate individuals. Another apparent advantage of the idea of poverty is that it appears more benevolent and caring than the abstract idea of "development." It is certainly more comforting, we must admit, than the concept of "economic coherence." Conversations about poverty seem to reach down into the difficult life prospects of individuals and households rather than focus attention on the impersonal aspects of national-level statistical data and indicators of economic performance. Fighting poverty evokes a purposeful commitment to the work of those engaged in development assistance. Unfortunately, actions and results rarely match terminology.

While donors do indeed undertake a number of valuable projects and programs under the banner of fighting poverty, it cannot be in doubt that the primary motivation for donor assistance is to bring about economic growth. Indeed, the current "new idea" in development assistance is called "growth diagnostics" in which great effort will be devoted to identifying market distortions as constraints on growth (Hausmann, Rodrik, and Velasco 2006). This focus on growth is reassuring to the donors and those who provide them with funding because "economic growth" is a central organizing principle of the highly industrialized countries that pay for development assistance. Of equal importance, a constant emphasis on growth suggests that the day will soon come when development assistance will no longer be necessary. Convergence will eliminate poverty.

With convergence, formerly poor countries will no longer be poor. That is, they will contain few, if any, poor individuals. When this happy state arrives, the elaborate structure and expense of donor assistance will no longer be necessary. Convergence will have put the donors out of business, and the financial commitments now expected from the wealthy industrial countries, small though they may be in percentage terms, will no longer be necessary. The political appeal of the convergence agenda is to be found in the expectation that as more countries "graduate" there will soon be only a very few who will require development assistance. With good work, those countries needing development assistance will gradually disappear.

Notice that there is an implied parallel process at work here. The logic of convergence stresses economic growth as the assured means to eliminate poverty, while the logic of fighting poverty enables donors to work on a variety of programs concerning poor people. This direct assistance to the poor will, it is assumed, launch them into the market and produce economic growth. Unfortunately, this dual-track strategy requires two presumptions—neither of which seems plausible.

The first presumption is that economic growth, measured as an increase in per capita GDP, will lift people out of poverty. The persistence of poverty and hunger among 20–23 percent of the world's inhabitants suggests that this presumption is not tenable (Kakwani and Son 2006; World Bank 2005b). To take an obvious example, as large deposits of oil are discovered and subsequently exported, total GDP will rise. When that larger indicator of total economic activity is divided by the total population, GDP per capita will be higher than previously. When that per capita GDP is then compared to the poverty line, it may well appear that poverty has been reduced. However, when the evidence from household living-standard surveys is compiled, it usually turns out that the prevalence of poverty has not changed at all. In other words, economic growth has not alleviated poverty. It may, but there is no guarantee that it will. This is certainly the case in Equatorial Guinea, Nigeria, and even Botswana—the latter country being held out as an African success story.

The second presumption is that programs to "fight poverty" play a significant role in bringing individuals (and households) into a sustainable relationship with promising market activity and that this engagement with the market will eventually yield increases in per capita GDP—a signal that economic growth has occurred. This presumption is also difficult to support.

To summarize our doubts, convergence does little to solve poverty, and fighting poverty does little to bring about convergence. It is from such doubts that we come to our emphasis on economic coherence. Countries advance economically and therefore socially when economic processes are coherent. The standard development approach, justified by enhancing economic growth, does not produce economic coherence. Indeed, in the case of the "resource curse," economic growth can render economies less coherent. Moreover, fighting poverty has little to do with creating economic coherence. The urgent development opportunity is not to fight poverty, nor is it to induce economic growth. Both of those outcomes are mere symptoms of economies that fail to function as they must if vulnerable people and vulnerable states are to be rescued from their malaise. Development assistance must turn its attention to the incoherencies in economic processes.

Implications

Creating economic coherence is a more promising and fruitful organizing principle for development assistance than pursing "growth" or "fighting poverty." Bringing economic coherence will solve the problems of vulnerable people and vulnerable states.

Virtually everyone in the developing world lives in poverty—that follows from the fact that those countries are not yet developed (they are "poor"). But not everyone in a developing country is vulnerable. Millions of individuals and families have viable agricultural pursuits, they own small (or large) businesses, they are engaged in a range of economic activities, and they are slowly building promising lives.

Our focus here on vulnerable people and vulnerable states offers insights concerning coherence—the processes by which economies become stuck on dynamic or asymptotic trajectories. National economies are the purposeful artifacts of policies that ordain one trajectory as opposed to another. Low-level economic torpor is avoided through conscious human volition and economic policies that focus on solving immediate problems. Dynamic economies are both responsive and adaptive. Asymptotic economies are neither.

Acknowledging the importance of vulnerability, and as the world financial situation deteriorated in early 2009, the World Bank announced the creation of a new "vulnerability fund." The purpose of this initiative was to remind the rich countries that there were many countries unable to mount meaningful economic recovery programs without the aid of foreign donors. The Bank was urging the developed world to devote 0.7 percent of their own economic stimulus packages to provide important assistance to infrastructure projects, additional safety-net programs (cash transfers for schooling and nutrition), and finance for small and medium-sized businesses. If those additional funds were indeed devoted to addressing problems of vulnerable people, then there is hope that their lives will be improved. And if that should happen, then the nations in which they live will also become less vulnerable. But these short-term ameliorative policies cannot serve as a substitute for the urgent need to create economic coherence.

3

CONTENDING WITH ECONOMIC INCOHERENCE

The notional state

Divergence in relative productivity levels and living standards is the dominant feature of modern economic history. In the last century, incomes in the "less developed" (or euphemistically, the "developing") countries have fallen far behind those in the "developed" countries, both proportionately and absolutely. I estimate that from 1870 to 1990 the ratio of per capita incomes between the richest and the poorest countries increased by roughly a factor of five and that the difference in income between the richest country and all others has increased by an order of magnitude. This divergence is the result of the very different patterns in the long-run economic performance of two sets of countries.

(Pritchett 1997: 3)

The problem

It is an article of faith among the development community that convergence is the natural state of affairs—that is, historical disparities in per capita incomes and living standards across the globe will disappear as the technology, the institutions, and the economic insights from the developed world make their way to the poorer countries.

The convergence conjecture underpins the establishment, following World War II, of the Bretton Woods organizations—the International Monetary Fund and the International Bank for Reconstruction and Development (the World Bank). Despite this general confidence in the logic of convergence, there is persistent evidence that the standard approaches to economic development—but especially in Africa—have brought disappointing results (Bigsten 2002; Easterly 2001, 2006, 2007; Easterly and Levine 1997; Herbst 2000; Leonard and Straus 2003; Ndulu and O'Connell 1999; Pritchett 1997; Rodrik 2003; Sender 1999; Tiffen 2003; van de Walle 2001). Indeed, much of the current frustration within the development discourse arises from the fact that a number of countries have somehow failed to go along with that presumption of convergence. What is wrong with them? Why can't they seem to get it right?

The Washington Consensus now seems discredited (Rodrik 2006; World Bank 2005b). It has been noted that "Results have been extraordinarily varied. In fact, what the experience of the past 15 years has shown is that policies that work wonders in one place may have weak, unintended, or negative effects in other places" (Hausmann, Rodrik and Velasco 2006: 1). And, as suggested earlier, it appears that many countries, most of them in Africa, will fail to meet the Millennium Development Goals by the year 2015. Several reasons are advanced for these discouraging circumstances: (1) lack of commitment by governments to implement and to persist in the development policies formulated for them; (2) unwillingness on the part of donors to advance a consistent development scenario in the face of shifting government priorities; (3) insufficient funding by donors to accomplish the desired development agenda; and (4) chronic corruption that undermines the effectiveness of even the most sensible development prescriptions.

THE WASHINGTON CONSENSUS

1. Fiscal discipline
2. Reorder public expenditure priorities
3. Tax reform
4. Liberalize interest rates
5. Competitive exchange rate
6. Trade liberalization
7. Liberalize foreign direct investment
8. Privatization
9. Deregulation
10. Property rights

Left unnoticed in the many reasons why development assistance has not produced better results is the possibility that development advice—the urgent and quite specific policy prescriptions—directed to particular nations on the African continent (as well as parts of the Middle East) is predicated on an inappropriate conceptual model of the actual process of economic development. In other words, if past and current development activities are predicated on a flawed understanding of the reasons why many nations seem resistant to the standard development catechism, the blame for failed development performance lies not with desultory governments, nor with endemic corruption, nor with inappropriate institutions. Nor is this failure the result of inadequate development funding. Rather, the disappointing development results lie with an inappropriate conceptual model that informs international development prescriptions and their associated assistance programs.

With this dubious development model intact, with little apparent interest in questioning its presumptions, and with little good to show for decades of billions of dollars spent on development assistance, the conversation now seems to have coalesced around two new strategies: (1) the great leap forward; and (2) smart searching. The first view is associated with Jeffrey Sachs (2005, 2008), while the second is associated with William Easterly (2006). Following Sachs requires that we are not in doubt about what is necessary and sufficient to induce self-sustaining growth and development—we must simply do more of it, and with a greater intensity of funds and technical assistance. Following Easterly also requires that we are not in doubt about the essential causal structure and implies that we need only to be more circumspect in our programmatic focus and emphasis. Easterly invokes the metaphor of the searcher as opposed to the planner.

As the previous chapter makes clear, our purpose here is to suggest that development progress in Africa, and to some extent elsewhere, is elusive not because of failed states or failed leadership. Rather, development has been elusive because of an inappropriate conceptual basis for the programs, projects, and policy prescriptions offered up as a guide to how countries ought to go about the process of achieving development. The wrong medicine is on offer because the reasons for the current dysfunction have never been properly diagnosed.

With particular reference to the African continent—where the vast majority of the vulnerable people and vulnerable states are to be found—development progress has suffered because much of the continent is characterized by what we call the *notional state*. The concept of notional states must not be confused with familiar accounts of corruption and failed states. Rather, the idea of notional states describes a situation in which the effective reach of the state is rationally attenuated— circumscribed—by both historic and contemporary considerations of the benefits and costs of extending effective governance, and therefore economic coherence, across vast landscapes of dubious economic value, and often devoid of very many people.

The concept of the notional state is not well understood in the development community because it differs from the common conception of the state as it is known among those who offer advice to governments. That shared idea of the state, implicit in standard models of development, is informed by familiarity with the process of nation building and the emergence of the state in Western Europe.

That specific history entails the emergence of strong states motivated to protect valuable agricultural assets that eventually underwrote the transition—epitomized by the Industrial Revolution—to the suite of highly developed economies. By the eighteenth century several of these strong states were in a military and financial position to impose this European idea—but not the empirical reality—of the state on a very different agro-ecological asset base. The "scramble for Africa" was the frantic effort by a number of European nations to stake out spheres of influence on the "dark continent" (Meredith 2005; Pakenham 1991). Unfortunately, the mere possession of such vast territories is not sufficient to launch the inhabitants of those places on a beneficial economic and political trajectory. In fact, the opposite result is now on display.

The actual realization of this idea of the European state failed to take hold in Africa because the inherent quality of the agricultural asset base is too meager to generate taxation that can support the necessary governance across space. As a result, the gradual establishment of the *empirical state* as it has emerged in more favorable ecological and economic settings turns out to be quite impossible. European colonialism left Africa with what we call juridical states—boundaries on a map—with little empirical content beyond the capital city. The same can be said of several Middle East states. Following independence, post-colonial governments have likewise found scant economic rationale to transform these juridical (notional) states into empirical states. The contemporary African state is optimally attenuated, and in this attenuation lie the roots of persistent economic incoherence.

The above claim warrants elaboration. Recall that the standard diagnosis is that the current poor countries are poor through mismanagement and corruption. In this view, economic dysfunction is the fault of corrupt or incompetent politicians. In contrast to this rather shallow political "explanation," we here offer an alternative hypothesis derived from economic theory. Specifically, governance—and the establishment of the necessary organizations and functions of government (offices, communications systems, record keeping)—are expensive undertakings. These countries are too poor to be able to extend the reach of government and governance across vast and mostly empty spaces. Our diagnosis suggests that such countries remain economically dysfunctional because of current political and economic circumstances arising out of both economic and historic circumstances.

It may appear that the fault lies with colonialism. However, we suggest that the very nature of colonialism in Africa and parts of the Middle East was itself dependent upon the same agro-ecological settings and circumstances that continue to create economic incoherence. Colonialism did not necessarily cause current dysfunction. Rather, colonialism operated as it did in Africa and the Middle East precisely because of these pre-existing conditions. The exact nature of colonialism in this part of the world is the result of those pre-existing conditions, not the reason for them.

Consider this explanation in greater detail. As we saw in Figures 2.1 and 2.2, the nature and evolution of economic systems is largely set in motion by the agro-ecological settings and circumstances in which a people are situated. It would be difficult indeed to imagine a viable agricultural or industrial economy emerging in Antarctica or Northern Siberia. We may think of these settings and circumstances as the resource set, or the asset base, that underwrites future material progress.[1] Central aspects of this resource set include climate, weather, soils, rainfall, solar energy, and wind. It is from within this complex of circumstances that people set about to feed and clothe themselves. And it is from this physical endowment that future technical and institutional change enables the gradual augmentation of provisioning.

The specific "getting and spending trajectories" are largely defined by these settings and circumstances (Kamarck 1976).

We do not suggest that these conditions pre-ordain any particular future material provisioning. Rather, the conditions merely make possible certain materialist strategies while precluding others. Of equal importance, political structures and the associated governance arrangements co-evolve with the livelihood strategies in each of these particular agro-ecological circumstances. Therefore, evolved governance processes, and indeed the nature of the political community (the state), are dependent on these circumstances. As an example, governance processes and the institutional (legal) aspects of collective decision making differed profoundly between a sedentary agricultural society in Western Europe and one that is dependent on pastoralism or transhumance as in the Middle East and Africa. The financial support for governance—and for the organizations of governance—also differs. Sedentary agriculture and industry offered a very different taxing regime in pre-industrial Europe from that found in a mobile pastoral economy of Africa. People who live in one place have different attitudes about paying for governance and governments than do those who make their living by moving. This explains the indifference—even hostility—that some governments display toward pastoralists.

From these considerations we can see that the nature of the state and its financial support become important variables in a diagnosis of economic dysfunction. In particular, we can predict two general models of the state emerging from these considerations.

The first, what we can call an empirical state, embodies the necessary structures and functions (and financial capacity) to provide coherent governance across the entire geographic reach of its alleged sovereignty. In feudal times, the lord (or king) projected governance across the entire geographic territory over which he ruled. Of course this is a tautology. Such people "ruled" only those territories they could possess and control. Over there, someone else ruled. In contemporary terms, the government of France effectively rules and governs over the entire domain we (and others) recognize as France. It has no writ in Belgium.

But European colonialism left a very different legacy in Africa and the Middle East. In those marginal regions, "nations" were carved out on maps quite without consideration for the economic and political structures that had evolved—at the point of a sword or cannon—back home. What we know as Switzerland or France or Denmark is the evolved manifestation of indigenous economic and political processes, not all of them pleasant, occurring over several thousand years. What we know as Ghana or Kenya or Angola is the handiwork of politicians and geographers at the Berlin Conference during the winter of 1894–95. The difference is profoundly important. The various "states" in Africa, and indeed the "states" of Pakistan, India, Afghanistan, Jordan, Syria, Iraq, and Saudi Arabia are the cartographer's gift of colonial meddling. These are not empirical states. Rather, they are notional states. They are "notional" because their creation is the result of artificial processes that wrought boundaries without compelling economic, cultural, or historic rationale.

Notional states cannot "get going" because they have no shared history to recall and therefore to summon up for defining a desired future. Governance is difficult because durable cultural memories adhere to other ideas. The economy atrophies because there cannot be a market economy in the absence of a cultural memory of a market society. Autarky is the predicted result.

These processes can be understood in the context of an economic model that provides an explanation for two kinds of states—the operational (empirical) state, and the notional (juridical) state. The notional states of the Middle East and Africa are geographic entities encompassing physical space of dubious economic value. Even the oil and other natural resources of such obvious economic value are small consolation of doubtful long-run benefit. The "resource curse" reminds us that these so-called gifts of nature are mere accidental endowments that bring forth scant investment, minimal employment, and a revenue stream that is easily captured by the ruling elite (Sachs and Warner 2001; Brunnschweiler and Bulte 2008).

Where natural assets are economically promising and widely spread across the space occupied by the state, there is obvious advantage in controlling those valuable spaces and projecting governance over them. This spatially distributed natural (though often latent) wealth provides a wide economic base for taxation. On the contrary, where natural assets are relatively worthless, as with much of the land in the Middle East and Africa, there is little interest in those assets and the geography they represent. More to the point, there is scant economic reason to incorporate those assets and their dubious income stream into the economic and political concerns of the state.

From the seventeenth to the nineteenth century, while most European nations were engaged in diplomacy and armed warfare over the geographic extent of their respective city-states—Rome, Paris, Berlin, London, Moscow, Vienna—some of them were also projecting political and military rule over Africa and the Middle East. For the most part, this interest was driven by a desire for the natural resources that could be extracted and sold on world markets, or shipped to Europe for domestic use. Copper, gold, diamonds, timber, and a few crops (cotton, tea, coffee, tobacco) were the objects of greatest interest. Throughout much of this time slaves were the dominant export from the African continent (Maddison 2007; Nunn 2008).

After World War II, when European nations finally lost interest in colonialism, the new independent governments inherited a tradition of governance that reflected the attenuated spatial reach of colonial administration. The stark differences between Europe, and the Middle East and Africa, in the inherent quality of the natural landscape explain these different governance strategies. Europe had a bounteous asset base worth fighting over and controlling, while the material circumstances in the arid regions around the Mediterranean and down into Africa represented vast domains largely devoid of compelling economic potential. European states grew strong in the eighteenth and nineteenth centuries because they had to be. African and Middle Eastern states in these years were weak because they had no reason to be strong. And so, at independence, political structures and processes were centered on the capital cities. Nearly five decades later, they remain that way (Herbst 2000).

These notional states were (and are) weak because, unlike those in Europe, they have never had compelling reasons to be strong. Individuals scattered across these meager landscapes are not the subjects of the governments and elaborate processes of governance. They are merely there—behind the mask of citizenship. Some scholars argue that Africa's political problems are examples of "personal rule" (Leonard and Straus 2003). This makes it sound as if despite feasible alternatives, ruthless despots have grabbed for themselves sole responsibility for governance. This claim confuses result with reasons. What looks like personal rule is the evolved result of historic processes that have now produced the only governance structure possible. These countries, handed at independence economically incoherent "national territory," now must work with the hand they have been dealt. Few of them hold winning hands.

The development challenge in a notional state

Our challenge to received development theory and practice rests on an analysis of the *asset-centered* logic of the empirical state in Western Europe as compared to the *city-centered* logic of the notional state in Africa and the Middle East. These two distinct logics—and histories—are central to how economic development has played out in the two places (Jackson and Rosberg 1982). The first task therefore is to understand how a "theory" of economic development derived from one of these logics (and historic processes) has then been deployed since the 1950s to justify specific development programs and projects in circumstances that differ so profoundly from those which provided the particularistic empirical basis for that received theory.

As above, the agro-ecological settings and circumstances from Western Europe gave rise to particularistic political and economic arrangements that reinforced the extraordinary importance of investing in and controlling land, both in specific locations as well as across relatively favorable locations. This broad-spectrum program of capital deepening then provided the economic foundation of the modern European nation-state. And the institutional arrangements associated with those gradually enhanced assets, including the tax bargain between owners and the state, provided a governance structure that bound scattered populations to their government (Moore 2007). The result is what we call the empirical state.

That is, these favorable agro-ecological settings gradually gave rise to an economy based on sedentary agriculture predicated on familiar Ricardian quality differentials. Coincident with this emergence of a particular agricultural economy, there evolved the need for correlated political arrangements dedicated to the protection of that augmented asset base with its embodied capital, and its politically "attached"—through elaborate land-centered property rights arrangements—labor and management of the owner. We call the end product of this evolutionary process *capitalist agriculture*.

It is capitalist agriculture because one person (or one family) was granted ownership over a specific parcel of this increasingly valuable asset base, and that owner was then free to contract with the large number of those who did not own land in order to bring their labor power to bear on the landed estate of the capitalist. The asset base explains the evolution of a particular ownership structure, and that ownership structure explains the evolution of the associated political and economic structures.

Notice that from this quite specific constellation of ecological, economic, and political circumstances, gradually forming the conditions upon which powerful nation-states might arise, economists have gradually built up a theory of the idea of economic development. If a country wishes for development it must replicate the process as interpreted from Western Europe—a process then replicated in a few other places (Southeast Asia comes to mind) that also possess, thanks to abundant water, favorable agro-ecological circumstances. This shared understanding of the processes by which the various nations of Western Europe evolved into modern industrial powers has underwritten the crafting of a theory of what others must do if they wish for a prosperous future. Such is the theory of economic development.

Peter Timmer (1990) has summarized the received theory of development, which—if not explicit in every World Bank Poverty Reduction Strategy Paper (PRSP)—is implicit therein. In the first stage emphasis must be placed on ridding the economy of distortions, on encouraging technical change, on the nurturing of markets for the movement of factors of production and the resulting outputs, and a major commitment must be made to improvements in rural infrastructure. A second stage sees the agricultural sector becoming more closely linked with the urban (industrial and service) economy, there is continuing pressure to improve technology in agriculture, and emphasis must be put on improving factor markets to mobilize rural resources. The third stage finds agriculture rather completely integrated with the emerging industrial sector. Urban consumers find that the share of their income devoted to food starts to fall—thereby freeing up disposable incomes for other urban investments. The pressure on agriculture to become even more efficient induces further replacement of labor with machinery, thus freeing rural labor to migrate to urban centers—providing a willing army of labor-power prepared to work at low wages. If rural incomes start to lag then some political remediation may be necessary. The journey is complete when agriculture eventually becomes a minor source of total national income. While agriculture may come to be a dominant engine of foreign exchange, it soon comprises a small part of total GDP.

Notice that there is no timeline associated with this process. In some countries it has taken centuries. In Japan and Korea, where the U.S. forced the process in the wake of war, it seems to have been accomplished in a generation or two. John Mellor summarized this process by saying that:

> Economic development is a process by which an economy is transformed from one that is dominantly rural and agricultural to one that is dominantly urban, industrial, and service-oriented in composition. The objectives of the process can be usefully categorized as increased social wealth, equity, and stability. But because these objectives require a diversification of the economy

away from agriculture (no high-income, equitable, stable nations have agriculture as their dominant activity), the process is one of major structural transformation.

(Mellor 1990: 70)

The question worth asking is whether or not this development model is a universal prescriptive law. If it is indeed a universal law of what development entails, and of how to bring it about, then the great leap forward of Jeff Sachs or the careful searching of Bill Easterly may yet turn out to be the correct recipe for Africa and the Middle East. On the other hand, if the historic settings and circumstances of Western Europe are the empirical basis for a highly particularistic understanding of economic development (and how to induce it), and if the settings and circumstances into which that derived theory is deployed in the service of replicating that quite specific empirical account differ substantially from the circumstances that underwrite that theory, a development strategy entailing "more of the same"—even if accompanied by more money, or even if applied more cleverly—is doomed to failure.

To make the point in a different way, if the logic and processes spelled out by Timmer and Mellor—and implicit in all development assistance programs—are nothing but a recapitulation of the historic pattern followed in Western Europe and a few other places sharing favorable agro-ecological circumstances, the applicability of that process for Africa and the Middle East—with a vastly different asset base and associated governance logic—is highly problematic.

Indeed, the implications of vastly different agro-ecological circumstances in Africa and the Middle East from those found in Western Europe during the emergence of strong states offers an opening to challenge the idea that there is but one universally applicable theory of development. Specifically, differences in the inherent quality of the asset base between Western Europe and the arid stretches of the Middle East and Africa offer a plausible explanation of the quite different structure of land ownership in the two settings. With this model in hand we can begin to see the flaw in many policy recommendations concerning property regimes. Indeed, most alleged "explanations" of these different institutional arrangements appeal to nothing more substantive than claimed "primitive" property rights that are both the result of, and the cause of, poverty. From there it is a specious leap to suggest that the property institutions must be altered in order to solve poverty (de Soto 2000).

The model offered here situates the emergence and evolution of property regimes, economic strategies, and governance in an agro-ecological context that invites reflection on economic reasons for what we observe out on the ground. To the extent that observed governance structures and institutional arrangements are the evolutionary entailment of these quite particular agro-ecological circumstances, development prescriptions urging the "modernization" of those particular institutional arrangements are logically flawed (Bromley 1991, 2008a, 2008b; Larson and Bromley 1990; Lund 2008; Migot-Adholla *et al.* 1991; Ouedraogo *et al.* 1996; Place and Hazell 1993; Platteau 1996; Sjaastad and Bromley 1997, 2000). Notice that if particular economic and social circumstances are not plausibly responsible for certain unwanted outcomes then policies that alter those circumstances are perverse in the extreme.

Moving to the political realm, the nature and quality of the agricultural assets in the Middle East and Africa suggest profound differences in the logic and spatial extent of governance. Moreover, when the asset base to which capital and labor is to be applied is of a kind that little lasting good can be realized from that investment, even the most committed improving land owner will adopt a different provisioning strategy. It will soon become evident that investing additional capital and labor in a specific parcel of land is not a feasible economic undertaking. Other things become evident as well. Extensive military efforts to prevent others colonizing a decidedly indifferent natural asset base seem not worth the cost. And so, with the recent exception of a few border struggles in the Horn of Africa, the continent throughout its history has been free of military campaigns by one country to expropriate the territory of another. The contrast with Western Europe is striking.

This also means that efforts by governments to extract taxes from individuals scattered across the meager landscape are generally not worth the trouble. In the absence of a serious commitment to particular parcels of land, and given the inability to raise much public revenue from those in control of these indifferent parcels, those who rule over these great spaces at the extensive margin find that they are unable to mobilize the means to defend such assets against others. Luckily, the indifferent quality—and minimal economic value—of the land renders those assets unattractive to others, and therefore expensive operations to acquire them are largely fruitless. Why fight over assets that have so little economic value? Land in much of Africa and parts of the Middle East is not worth the trouble to acquire, nor is it worth the trouble to defend should others—for non-economic reasons—decide to expropriate it from those now in possession.

Note that these circumstances have given rise to economic strategies that place great value in mobility across space. We see a mixed agricultural economy—small-scale crop production, some livestock rearing, and a correlated commitment to the cultivation of social networks near and far. This extensification strategy leads to the evolution of political arrangements and governance structures that are supportive of a broad-spectrum survival program. For example, property regimes differ profoundly from those which evolved in Western Europe (Baland and Platteau 1996; Bromley 1991; Sjaastad and Bromley 1997, 2000). As above, seeing no need to be regional military powers, many African states are weak in comparison to states elsewhere in the world. African states are relatively weak because they have not had to be strong.

Consider the contrast with what we know of Western Europe.

> ...starting in the fifteenth century in Italy and later elsewhere, population densities increased...[and] European nations began to compete for territory, a tendency that only makes sense if population densities are relatively high and vacant land is limited or nonexistent...In turn, there was significant pressure

> to strengthen states in order to fight wars...Because European states were forged with iron and blood, it was critical for the capital to physically control its hinterland...Successful European state development was therefore characterized by profound links between the cities—the core political areas—and the surrounding territories. Indeed, the growth of states was closely correlated with the development of significant urban areas.
>
> *(Herbst 2000: 13–14)*

Herbst goes on to point out that it was not until 1975 that Africa recorded the sort of population densities common in Europe in 1500. In Africa, the current states were created long before many of the capital cities had developed beyond large towns. Europeans, in their African colonizing, relied on urban areas but the majority of these were on the coasts where they served the extractive interests of colonial administrators rather than those in the rural interior. Herbst continues:

> Due to low population densities and the large amount of open land in Africa, wars of territorial conquest...have seldom been a significant aspect of the continent's history. In precolonial Africa, the primary object of warfare...was to capture people and treasure, not land which was available to all...African leaders mainly exploited people outside their own polity because the point of war was to take women, cattle, and slaves. Thus the slave trade, especially in the eighteenth century, should be seen as part of the process by which African states grew: by capturing people rather than by gaining control over territory.
>
> *(Herbst 2000: 20–21)*

With political and economic relations predicated on the nature and extent of underlying economic assets, it seems reasonable that an asset-centric survival program would give rise to an emphasis on continual investments for the purpose of increasing the quantity and quality of labor and capital applied to particular parcels of Ricardian space. However, if the inherent asset base is poor, and only grudgingly yields payoff from investments in technology and agricultural know-how then other economic strategies will recommend themselves. It soon becomes evident that investing in specific parcels of land is a less rational economic strategy than investing in those activities that enhance economic prospects when it is necessary to move about. Think of this alternative program as an economy predicated on loose but durable social networks.

Implications

The paradox is complete. Desultory agro-ecological settings and circumstances in Africa (and the Middle East) have given rise to a household economic program that rewards extensification (mobility) over intensification (stationarity). The minimal economic value attributable to land offers a reason why African governments have had little reason to show much interest in the hinterland. And by showing little interest in the impecunious hinterland there is no reason for African governments to expect those individuals scattered across such vast spaces to hold the national government in much esteem. The economic estrangement is reciprocal. Those far from the center get nothing from the central government, and they give nothing to it. And the center, getting little in the way of tangible benefit from occupants of the hinterland, find few good reasons to pay them any attention. It is here that the mask of citizenship offers a clearer idea of the problem than the appeal to "personal rule." If we anchor Africa's development problems on the predominance of personal rule it conjures up the traditional images of tribalism, payoffs, and corruption. This avenue suggests that African culture must be destroyed or reformed before development can get underway.

On the other hand, if we understand the economic origins of the mask of citizenship it shifts the reasons for observed governance arrangements away from some allegedly defective African cultural trait and situates those reasons in the realm of economics and the "rationally attenuated" (notional) state. This is a much more promising basis for the necessary political reforms that can begin to underpin much-needed economic reforms. The pertinent question then becomes: What can be done in such circumstances to create the conditions in which economic progress is possible?

4

CREATING COHERENCE

The role of institutions

> ...the renewed interest in institutions on the part of many economists can be
> recognized as a growing conviction that satisfactory understanding of economic
> performance requires going beyond the lean logic of...stripped down neoclassical
> theory.
>
> (Nelson and Sampat 2001: 32)

This quote captures a popular sentiment among those who work in the area of
economic development—institutions matter. Unfortunately, there is no clear understanding of what, exactly, institutions are, or what they do. One sees reference to
institutional roles, institutional capacity, institutional rules, good and bad institutions,
efficient institutions, inefficient institutions, imperfect institutions, institutional
strengthening, and legal institutions. It is not very helpful to insist that institutions
matter when there are so many conflicting notions of institutions afoot. Our goal in
this chapter is to offer clarity as to the meaning—and the specific economic role—
of institutions. This is necessary if economic coherence is to be created.

Institutions: the legal foundation of an economy

For our purposes here, it is useful to suggest that institutions take two general forms:
(1) norms and conventions; and (2) legal (codified) rules (Bromley 1989a, 2006).
Norms and conventions, obviously important for development activities and outcomes, are generally informed by custom—what we might call cultural traditions.
These institutional arrangements, because of their cultural embeddedness, are rarely
the subject of explicit development activity. Of course they are important to development outcomes.

If the norm in a particular nation-state is that girls may not attend school beyond
a certain age then obviously particular development activities will be profoundly

influenced by this tradition. If the norm is that daughters cannot marry outside of the village then we should not be surprised to see particular modes of production and reproduction in rural areas. If partible inheritance of agricultural land is the norm in one region of a country, while primogeniture prevails elsewhere, we should not be surprised to see agricultural structures in the two regions within the same nation-state. How does the matter of tenure security relate to economic activity (Sjaastad and Bromley 1997, 2000)? If male and female children are differentially valued in particular cultures then political and economic pressure—and the resulting institutional arrangements with respect to family size—can be expected to make life unpleasant for new-born females.

LEGAL INSTITUTIONS AND POLICY REFORM

The institutions pertinent to development are the legal relations in a nation-state that define realms of acceptable and unacceptable individual behavior. An economy is constituted by this institutional architecture. Public policy is concerned with modifications in these legal arrangements with the explicit purpose of altering existing individual behaviors. Those behaviors are in need of modification because, in the aggregate, they lead to unwanted outcomes.

Policy reform is simply the process of modifying existing institutional arrangements.

We do not spend much time here on norms and conventions because, while they obviously matter for development programs and outcomes, they do not present themselves to the development assistance community as policy variables. However, because institutions matter for development outcomes, it is essential that there be clarity about which class of institutions warrant analytical attention. Only then will it be possible to assess the plausible efficacy of development activities and policy reform undertaken with that purpose in mind.

It is the legal institutions that are the object of policy reform of an economy (Bromley 1989b, 1991, 2006). These institutions are the collectively determined rules indicating what

> ...individuals *must* or *must not* do (compulsion or duty), what they *may* do without interference from other individuals (privilege or liberty), what they *can* do with the aid of collective power (capacity or right), and what they *cannot* expect the collective power to do in their behalf (incapacity or liability).
>
> *(Commons 1924: 6)*

Notice the presence here of a "collective power"—what we shall call *authoritative agents*. The authoritative agents of such importance to development are governments struggling to manage economies in the notional states discussed in Chapter 3. That is, the institutions of concern here are the formal and codified legal rules issued by legislatures, courts, and administrative agencies as part of the policy-making process common to all nations. These are the essential aspects of coherence that are missing in notional states.[1]

If an individual has a *right* then the individual possesses the legitimate (the socially sanctioned) capacity to compel the coercive power of the state (the pertinent authoritative agent) to come to the defense of that individual's specific interests. Notice that if the authoritative agent did not wish for the individual to have that capacity then that capacity—that right—would not have been granted to the individual in the first place (Becker 1977; Bromley 1991; Williams 1977). Once granted, the ability of the right holder to enlist the compulsive threat of the collective authority (the state) constitutes a correlated *duty* on others. To have a right means that you do not have to impose and self-enforce duties on others—authoritative agents have already agreed, when they granted you a right, to do that for you.[2]

Many problems arise because of a situation of "no law." In strict terms, this means that many settings are depicted by the legal correlates of *privilege* and *no right*. Under this institutional regime, particular individuals are free to act without regard for the implications to fall on others. If the workplace is entirely unregulated then owners are free (at liberty) to impose their will on individuals who work there. The history of labor unions has been a constant struggle to impose limits on the capacity (the exercise of privilege) of owners and managers to treat workers in an arbitrary and capricious manner.

AUTHORITATIVE AGENTS

The authoritative agents in a nation-state are those entities granted the ability to alter the institutional setup. In most countries, the authoritative agents would be legislatures, courts, and the administrative branches of government.

The police and the military are not authoritative agents since neither entity has the ability (in most countries) to alter the institutional architecture of the nation state. The police and the military have the tasks of enforcing the rules (the institutions) promulgated by legislatures, courts, and administrative agencies.

Must workers be given breaks and holidays? How many hours per week must they be made to work? Are they covered by old-age insurance? What if workers are injured in a workplace accident and are crippled for life? Is there a worker's compensation program to protect them and their families? May workers be dismissed without cause? Are there official grievance procedures?

These two legal correlates—right/duty and privilege/no right—comprise the essential institutional reality of all economic systems. When it is alleged that institutions matter for development it must be understood that the particular legal relations under discussion here matter profoundly for the process of development and for development outcomes. In many societies young people have a right to attend school up to a certain age, and their parents are under a legal duty to make sure that their children are indeed in school rather than in the workplace. Such laws protect children from short-sighted parents and from unscrupulous owners of firms. Notice that a law prohibiting child labor differs from a law requiring that all children be in school until the age of, say, 16. The first institution (rule) indicates what must not occur (child labor), while the second institution indicates what must occur (children in school rather than in the work place). Notice, as well, that the first rule allows children to roam the streets (though not work), while the second law prohibits children to roam the streets while school is in session.

In some countries industrial polluters may have a legal standing of privilege thereby allowing them to discharge their wastes into lakes and rivers without regard for the damages visited on others. This situation of legalized indifference to the harms imposed on others puts the victims in a situation of no right. Those harmed by pollution have no right to make polluters stop such practices. In other countries farmers and loggers have the right to destroy particularly valuable natural habitats, while those seeking protection of such sites have a duty not to interfere with those actions. If local or national groups should try to interfere with these logging activities, they can expect the local authorities to come to the defense of the loggers. In certain settings, farmers at the head of an irrigation system have privilege with respect to taking as much water as they desire, while farmers at the tail-end of such systems have no right with respect to water allocation. These legal correlates are depicted in Table 4.1.

We see that a right means that one individual (Alpha) has a state-sanctioned and enforced expectation and assurance that another person (Beta) will behave in a certain way toward Alpha. A duty means that Beta must behave in a specific way with respect to Alpha. Notice that the dual of Alpha's legal position is Beta's legal

TABLE 4.1 The legal correlates

	Alpha ←	→ Beta
Static Correlates	Right ←	→ Duty
	Privilege ←	→ No right
Dynamic Correlates	Power ←	→ Liability
	Immunity ←	→ No power

Source: Bromley 2006

position; Alpha has the right and Beta has the duty. On the other hand, if Alpha has privilege with respect to Beta then she (Alpha) is free to act without regard for the implications that may befall Beta from that action. As above, Alpha might be the head-end farmer in an irrigation system, while Beta—the tail-end farmer—stands in a position of no right to Alpha's privilege. If Beta seeks relief from this situation in a court of law he would be told that there is "no law" against Alpha's actions. Beta has no rights.

THE PROFUSION OF "RIGHTS TALK"

The word "rights" is frequently invoked in the hope of giving the speaker an advantage in a discussion concerning particular desired outcomes (Glendon 1991).

It will be declared that the speaker has a "right to…" by which it is better to understand that the speaker is declaring that she has an interest in doing something and she very much hopes that her use of the word "right" will carry a little extra weight in the discussion. One cannot have a "right" to anything unless the pertinent authoritative agent has agreed to impose binding duties on all others who have different ideas about desired actions and/or outcomes.

The lower half of Table 4.1 depicts the dynamic aspect to these legal relations. To have power is to have the ability to force other individuals into a new legal situation against their will. In economic terms, power is the ability to force another to suffer a loss of utility by the imposition of a new legal rule. If Alpha has power then she is able to draw on the coercive power of some authoritative agent (village headman, the central government) to impose her will on Beta's choice domain (field of action). The state (or the pertinent authority system) becomes an essential (a necessary) participant in the exercise of Alpha's power with respect to Beta. When Alpha has power, Beta suffers from a liability to the capacity of Alpha to force Beta into a new and unwanted legal situation. If Beta is not exposed to Alpha's attempt to create a new legal relation inimical to Beta's interests, then we say that Beta enjoys immunity in the face of Alpha's efforts to put Beta in an unwanted legal position. And in the face of Beta's immunity we would say that Alpha has no power. To have no power means that Alpha is unable to put Beta in a new legal situation contrary to the interests of Beta.

A special case of these legal rules concerns property relations. These property relations rest on the same structure of correlates (right/duty, privilege/no right) discussed above in the context of the working rules of the economy. The category of property relations concerns socially sanctioned and protected income (or benefit) streams arising from particular valuable objects such as land, or circumstances such as trademarks, copyrights or patents. Property relations—along with what have come to be called *civil rights*—are fundamental social relations among members of a political community (a nation-state). While civil rights laws are entitlements concerning the expected behaviors of all members of a polity towards each other, property relations concern collective assurance among members of the polity with respect to particular income (or special benefit) streams.

To have a right with respect to a particular activity (say the right to free assembly or to free speech) is to have the capacity to compel the state to protect your ability to assemble or to speak. To have a right with respect to a stream of future economic benefits is to have the capacity to compel the state to protect your control over that income stream—and to indemnify you from the treasury if that income stream is compromised in some way. The first of these we call a civil right. The second of these we call a *property right*. Note that property rights obtain their empirical content from the imposition by the state—or a comparable authority system—of a duty on all others not to interfere with the income stream accruing to the owner of the object or circumstances so protected.

The empirical reality of property relations is that they situate all members of a specific nation-state in a particular position with respect to valuable assets and circumstances regarded by the political community as warranting special protection. Settings and circumstances are not protected by the collective authority because they are property. Rather, settings and circumstances come to have rights associated with them—they become property—because the political community has determined that they warrant this special protection of the collective authority. The empirical content of ownership is the socially sanctioned ability to be the exclusive beneficiary of an income stream, and thus to have the correlated ability to compel the collective authority to protect your income stream in those circumstances. A copyright prevents others from benefiting at the expense of the creator. A patent gives temporary (often a finite period of time) protection to the inventor. Private property in land and other related assets sanctions socially legitimate exclusion of others (Bromley 1991). The Irish potato famine was not the result of the absence of food grown in Ireland. Rather, English landowners found it in their interest to send wheat back to the mother country rather than to make it available to their Irish tenants. And so when the potato blight struck, the Irish lost their only source of calories. Table 4.2 provides a summary of the ideas of rights, property, and property rights.

The economic role of institutions

To summarize, institutions define—demarcate—acceptable and unacceptable domains of individual action. Public policy—and policy reform—is concerned with the collective redefinition of domains of individual action so that altered behaviors might produce altered social and economic outcomes. That is what policy reform does. That is the purpose of policy reform.

TABLE 4.2 Rights, property, and property rights

Rights
Rights allow an individual to *compel* the coercive power of the state to come to her assistance. Rights do not entail passive support by the state but rather active assistance for those with rights. That is, the state stands ready to be enlisted in the cause of those to whom it has granted rights. We say that rights *expand the capacities* of the individual by indicating what one *can do with the aid of the collective power* (Bromley 1989a, 1991; Macpherson 1973; Commons 1924).

Property
Property is not an object but is instead, a *value*. When one buys a piece of land (in the vernacular, a "piece of property") one acquires not merely some physical object but rather *control over a benefit stream arising from that setting and circumstance that runs into the future*. That is why one spends money (one benefit stream) in order to acquire a different benefit stream ("ownership" of a new benefit stream arising from the fact of ownership). Notice that the magnitude of that new benefit stream is a function of the legal parameters associated with it. The price paid to acquire that new benefit stream is none other than the expected discounted present value of all future net income appropriable from "owning" the thing. This is why property is the *value*, not the object (Bromley 1991; Macpherson 1973, 1978).

Property Rights
Property rights bring together legal concepts of *rights* and *duties* with settings and circumstances (including objects) capable of producing income (Becker 1977; Bromley 1989a, 1991; Christman 1994; Hohfeld 1917). Property rights parameterize the nature and extent of income appropriable from control of income-producing settings and circumstances. Trademarks, copyrights, and patents are forms of property rights. All are forms of rights in property (the future value), and duties for non-owners.

This realization supports the understanding that it is impossible for countries to make gains in economic performance in the absence of a coherent strategic role on the part of its government. National governments are the essential catalytic agent in the creation of a plausible development strategy. If governments are not working well the appropriate response is not to lecture them to adopt "efficient institutions" or to "wise up." Rather, efforts must be devoted to help governments become better at addressing the problems faced by vulnerable individuals and households. And there must be more emphasis on institutional (policy) reform to enhance the capabilities of vulnerable states. These necessary steps are not possible when the dominant mantra is that the primary task of development is to "fight poverty."

If there is to be success in the quest for development among the remaining poor countries of the world, that success will necessarily come through programs to strengthen governments and their capacity for governance. And the central dimension of this need to strengthen governments and governance is concerned with policy reform. We earlier stressed that the essence of policy reform is found in the need for governments to implement an enduring strategy that accomplishes three purposes: (1) creating a well-functioning national market; (2) enhancing that national

ENABLING MARKETS

There is an important difference between enabling markets to work for the benefit of the development process, and insisting that markets are the solution to all development problems. When countries set specific development goals and objectives, and then enlist the beneficial aspects of market processes, it will generally work to good effect.

On the other hand, an insistence on markets in the absence of clarity about what those markets are supposed to do for the development process will often lead to problems. It must be kept in mind that markets are a means, not an end.

Development is enhanced to the extent that markets can be enabled rather than imposed.

market as it continues to evolve; and (3) supporting that national market over time as new exigencies (problems) arise. These ideas should not be seen as an endorsement of the "growth-first" approach to development. Rather, they address the important matter of economic coherence as a necessary strategy to nudge economies off of asymptotic trajectories and on to dynamic trajectories.

An economy is best understood as a structured set of implicit or explicit contractual relations among independent agents (Cheung 1983; Simon 1991). The central problem of economic organization—and the fundamental challenge to which governments must attend—is to design a process in which incentives and sanctions will guide individuals to act in the interest of the larger community. It is relatively easy to see that individuals will act in their own self-interest. It is a greater challenge to make sure that self-interested behavior also redounds to the benefit of others. Markets provide signals to individuals seeking jobs, commodities, or other opportunities, and to firms concerning the labor market, supplies, output prices, and other considerations. But markets, if they are to offer useful and facilitative signaling, must function with low transaction costs. Transaction costs entail the costs of obtaining information about possible market opportunities, the costs of negotiating contracts or bargains, and the costs of enforcing bargains or contracts that have been consummated.

A vibrant and flourishing national economy requires low-cost economic signaling, and such an economy requires frequent policy innovation to insure that transaction costs are kept low. For the most part, the economies of sub-Saharan Africa are domains of high transaction costs and these costs stifle needed economic initiative (Bromley 2008a; Bromley and Chavas 1989; Bromley and Foltz 2011). Similarly, the command economies of Eastern Europe were burdened with very high information costs, very high contracting costs, and very high enforcement costs. In such circumstances poor economic performance was virtually assured.

Clarity concerning the role of markets in economic development comes from the understanding that market economies—when they work well—solve the problem of mutual interdependence among individuals faced with localized abundance. Many people suppose that markets are animated by scarcity. In fact markets are driven by abundance in the hands of individuals who wish to trade some of their momentary abundance for something they do not have. In an economy of ubiquitous scarcity there is no incentive to trade. That is what we mean by a subsistence economy. Without localized abundance no one is willing or able to enter the market. Hence the first step in any development process must be to develop the means to facilitate the production and disposition of localized abundance.

A market economy consists of various opportunities for the willful exchange of ownership of benefit streams. The successful buyer turns over one benefit stream—currency—in exchange for another benefit stream—some object of greater benefit than the currency being sacrificed. Both buyer and seller must be presumed to gain net benefits from the transaction or it would not have occurred. But of course not all such exchanges recommend themselves to economists. Exchanges in which information is seriously asymmetric do not conduce to overall economic efficiency. Exchanges in which economic power is drastically asymmetric conduce neither to efficiency nor to equity. Exchanges in which large shares of the potential benefits are consumed by contracting or enforcement costs are not efficient and—depending on the incidence of such costs—may be far from equitable. Exchanges conducted under duress are not regarded as particularly compelling to economists. In other words, not all transactions (exchanges) are equal.

CREATING LOCAL ABUNDANCE

The development challenge can be thought of in terms of creating the settings and circumstances through which local livelihoods can be enhanced by the creation of local abundance. That abundance could be in terms of agricultural produce, it could be in terms of small manufactures, it could be in terms of a willing and eager labor force, it could be in terms of compelling natural environments, etc.

This local abundance becomes the necessary condition by which trade with other localities becomes possible—and thus new income streams might be engendered. These conditions do not arise overnight. They must be encouraged, and they must be nurtured through local initiatives and hard work.

Market transactions that commend themselves to economists are those that occur in "efficient" markets. An efficient market is one in which all participants have approximately the same information, no participant is in a monopoly position to influence prices, and the resulting transaction is not accompanied by high contracting and enforcement costs that must be borne by market participants. We say that the share (or stock) market is an efficient market. Commodities and futures markets are also thought to be efficient markets. These markets bring buyers and sellers together and the prices paid in such markets represent the very best expectations of both participants—conditioned only on the differences in individual subjective valuations of the things being exchanged.

Such markets, as seen above, have informational attributes, contracting attributes, and enforcement attributes. We discuss each of these.

Informational attributes

The information attributes of markets address those aspects of the objects or circumstances being exchanged around which market participants form their expectations about the virtues of an exchange. To the seller, only one thing matters—the legal standing of the currency being offered by the buyer. That is, is this cash real or counterfeit? Is this check backed by funds in a credible bank? Does this credit card have the backing of the company that owns the card? The buyer usually has a more daunting information problem. Is this product reliable? Is this vendor reliable? What is the expected life of this product? Will I like it as much tomorrow as I do today? Are there hidden flaws in design or implementation? What happens if it turns out to be flawed? Can I get my money back?

These considerations remind us that markets can only work well—conduce to efficiency—if there are low-cost ways to provide both parties to a transaction with credible information about the merits of any particular transaction. The successful buyer will wonder if she picked the right seller. The successful seller will wonder what the next best buyer might have offered. The unsuccessful seller will wonder if he should have lowered his price a bit. The unsuccessful buyer will wonder if he should have offered a tiny bit more. Efficient markets have the characteristic that there is little if any post-transaction regret. As with a super-fair game, we may say that efficient markets are characterized by the absence of envy once the transaction is complete; no participant would wish to trade places with any other participant, or would wish the transaction annulled.

Contracting attributes

Many transactions, and particularly those implied above, represent one-off opportunities in which buyer and seller come together momentarily for the purpose of the transaction and in the next instant the deal is consummated. We might think of these as *spot markets*. In such transactions contracting costs tend to be low. Money—or a comparable instrument—is exchanged for an object or circumstance of equal or greater value and nothing more is called for.

However, some transactions bind parties together over an extended period of time and here contracting costs can be important considerations in how markets work.

If you join a private club you exchange money for a long-term benefit stream—the full nature of which may not become apparent until some time has elapsed. The club has your money but you have not yet received the full array of benefits to flow from the fees you paid. In such transactions, a variety of "contractual" relations exist that will specify the conditions under which both parties enter into the transaction. Similarly, if you contract with a carpenter to make modifications to your home, you engage someone in a transaction that has a distinct time element at the core of the exchange. In a sense the transaction can be thought of as a *relational contract* that keeps both parties engaged in an ongoing process of negotiation.

Efficient markets tend to have low contracting costs, where the notion of "low" means that all feasible contingencies are agreed to at the time of the initial engagement, and both parties commit to good-faith re-contracting as time plays out. Like the concept of "bounded rationality," the concept of "low contracting costs" begs the question of when enough information exists to engage in time-mediated transactions. However, as an empirical matter, we can develop guidelines for "low" contracting costs by making reference to various market transactions where time is a central factor.

Enforcement attributes

High enforcement costs render some transactions infeasible. In such settings, potentially beneficial transactions never take place and valuable exchanges are stifled. The literature on transaction costs refers to transactions that must be "privately ordered." *Private ordering* means that the individual transactors must (privately) enforce all of the terms of the transaction (Williamson 2002, 2005). Private ordering is expensive for the simple reason that it fails to enjoy the considerable economies of scale that come with a coherent national-level legal system. Instead of a judicial system that stands ready to enforce all transactions, each transactor must retain and remunerate his or her own means of enforcement. While one might suppose that competition among the private-ordering sector would hold prices down, the very existence of such private enforcers reveals the absence of a collective apparatus to prevent extortion. In fact, collusion often leads to price escalation in the face of indifferent performance. Privately ordered markets are not efficient markets. Efficient markets rely on the collective good that is a civil society and here the legal structures and procedures provide for low-cost enforcement of all transactions. Indeed a coherent legal system provides a credible threat that results in compliance without the necessity of enforcement.

Implications

Existing institutions are the result of prior collective action that was formulated with particular reasons (purposes) in mind. These existing institutional arrangements constitute the legal parameters that liberate and restrain individual action. As we know, the sum total of individual action will, from time to time, result in particular social, economic, or environmental outcomes that no longer seem desirable. As above, these circumstances relegate countries to asymptotic trajectories. If those institutional arrangements can be rectified, it is possible to nudge countries on to dynamic trajectories. We see that the development enterprise must be concerned with the careful identification of unwanted economic and social outcomes in countries that are themselves poor. And there must be careful focus on the reasons and causes for those unwanted outcomes.

In this regard, the purpose of policy reform—institutional change—is to undertake incremental improvements in ongoing economic processes that determine which trajectory will be followed. Policy reform is best thought of as a process of gradualism in which governments identify key leverage points where feasible policy reforms offer promising and sustainable payoffs. The central idea here is *leverage* for the simple reason that coherent policy reform must use existing governance structures and protocols to address problems that have been identified by citizens or government officials. National governments will need to rely on *policy entrepreneurs* to help define pressing problems, to help work out plausible solutions to those problems, and then to help implement feasible changes that stand a reasonable chance of success. Policy reform is not as noticeable as building dams or highways or schools. Policy reform is process oriented.

We now turn to a more specific discussion of exactly how and why existing institutions are instrumental to unwanted social outcomes.

5

POLICY REFORM AS INSTITUTIONAL INNOVATION

...the canonical ideas of orthodox microeconomic theory obscure essential features of the processes of economic change. The insistence on strict "maximization" in orthodox models makes it awkward to deal with the fact that, in coping with exogenous change and in trying out new techniques and policies, firms have but limited bases for judging what will work best; they may even have difficulty establishing the range of plausible alternatives to be considered...Over time the least satisfactory of the responses...may tend to be eliminated and the better of the responses may tend to be used more widely, but...these selection forces take time to work through. Since orthodox microeconomic theory is based on the ideas that firms maximize and that the industry...is in equilibrium...models built according to the orthodox blueprints miss completely or deal awkwardly with these features of economic change.

(Nelson and Winter 1982: 399–400)

Introduction

Our emphasis on policy reform recognizes the central importance of institutions in understanding and explaining individual behaviors. And of course social outcomes are the inevitable consequences of a multitude of individual behaviors. A policy problem arises when particular unwanted social outcomes become apparent—think of them as "social irritants"—and, as a result, there emerges a growing consensus that those outcomes must be rectified. Central to this process is recognition of the need for a diagnostic undertaking that will help to identify the plausible causes of these unwanted outcomes. The diagnostic endeavor would necessarily focus on the existing institutional arrangements that provide the plausible reasons for—offer an explanation of—those observed behaviors. Once we have isolated those institutional reasons it is possible to initiate a process that will lead to the modification of those implicated institutions under the expectation that doing so will bring forth altered (better) individual, and therefore more beneficial aggregate, behaviors. And of course the reason for altering individual and aggregate behaviors is precisely to generate more desired social outcomes in the future.

Notice that many observers will blame prices—economic incentives—for the unwanted outcomes. They will want to "get prices right." We certainly agree that incentives motivate choices and actions. But prices must be understood as the result of the legal underpinnings of an economy, combined with past choices made in specific arenas of exchange. On the legal front, if firms must pay taxes on the labor they hire—contribute to health benefits, or to unemployment compensation—then the "price" of labor is not merely the hourly wage received by the employee, but it also must include the extra cost of "fringe benefits" for which firms are responsible. We might think of these added costs as "payroll taxes" on hired labor. Moreover, today's prices are dependent on what has recently happened in a particular market. In that sense prices are both resultants of "yesterday's" transactions, as well as signals that will inform "tomorrow's" transactions. We see that getting prices "right" necessarily entails addressing the underlying institutional scaffolding on which market transactions rest, and also understanding the conditions—past, present, future—likely to bring about fluctuations in prices at any moment.

As a necessary precursor to Chapter 6 concerning diagnostics, here we focus attention on the evolution of institutional arrangements in an economy. The approach taken starts from a broader perspective on the development challenge than does the standard development model. That is, the standard view starts from the notion that economics is the study of the rational allocation of scare resources by maximizing agents in their quest to meet unlimited wants (Boyes and Melvin 2005; Mankiw 2007). Indeed, adherence to this narrow approach often comprises a short-hand notion of the central organizing idea of contemporary economics.

We find this approach to be overly restrictive. Since it is the canonical mental lens through which development economists have been trained, it cannot be a surprise that this narrow approach is foundational to how the development challenge is per-ceived, and how it is implemented by the donor agencies. By way of contrast, we insist that economics—if it is to be useful to the development enterprise—must be understood as the science that is concerned with how societies organize themselves for their material provisioning. With this broader vision available to development practitioners, it soon becomes apparent that economics is best understood as a sci-ence not of choice but a *science of consequences*. The difference warrants elaboration.

When economics is thought of as the application of rational choice models to problems of ubiquitous scarcity, analytical attention is devoted to the process of market transactions and individual maximization. When things do not work well the blame will immediately be found to lie with some alleged "market failure." This then leads to a search for flawed price signals, and the perverse behavior of politi-cians—too easily labeled corruption—who stifle the otherwise beneficent wonders of the so-called "free market." Notice that this approach leaves aside any interest in how and why existing scarcities—the social facts (*Data* in Figures 2.1 and 2.2) that necessitate choice in the first place—came to be.

When particular scarcities are taken for granted—when they are thought of as constraints—their pertinence to the development problem is ignored. Recall that much of the reason why poor countries are poor is that existing scarcities—access to good agricultural land, access to other natural resources, access to plausible employment prospects—are often the result of an institutional structure that creates landlessness, economic marginalization, and a labor force with minimal education and few job skills. The process of economic development is most assuredly not an exercise in improving the allocation of scarce resources within this flawed institutional structure. Rather, successful development interventions require a careful diagnosis of which institutional arrangements give rise to particular economic circumstances—artificial scarcities and barriers—that then preclude enhanced social and economic outcomes for the vast majority of citizens.

If one wishes to understand why so many people in the developing world are exceedingly poor—hence giving rise to "poor countries"—one must first understand the specific institutional structures that stand as the plausible reasons for that outcome. Poor people (and poor countries) are the quite expected result of flawed institutional arrangements that conspire to assure that a small group of individuals, well served by that institutional structure, are not poor. Even in the poorest countries of sub-Saharan Africa some individuals are doing quite well indeed. What is it about existing institutional arrangements that gives rise to such outcomes?

When economics is understood as the science of consequences then development diagnosis starts with questions about why particular scarcities seem to arise, and to persist. We see here a diagnostic approach to the consequences of existing institutions that underlie particular material conditions against which individual maximizing behavior must occur. In more specific (technical) terms, if the production possibilities frontier (PPF) could be understood as an artifact of particular institutional arrangements then the obvious question of how to solve serious economic problems among participants in the economy would necessarily focus on why that PPF is situated as it is—and whose interests are well served by its exact construction (Bromley 1995). It is not in doubt that landlordism and landless tenancy in a particular country define (situate) the pertinent PPF. Nor can it be denied that an agricultural structure in which landlordism is absent and farmers are independent entrepreneurs—with access to credit, necessary inputs, and with plausible market channels for needed inputs and outputs—would yield a dramatically different PPF. Notice that this broader conception of economics focuses attention on policy reform as part of the necessary process of considering the social construction of pertinent scarcities. The location and properties of the PPF are not divinely given—they are the result of certain institutions and processes.

What are these processes? What are the reasons for their persistence? Whose interests are thereby advanced? What are the impediments, economically and politically, to a redefinition (a reconstitution) of those existing constraints? Which socially constructed scarcities can be most expeditiously overcome? This diagnostic approach is central to understanding economics as an evolutionary science preoccupied with consequences.

Evolutionary institutional change

Policy reform must be understood as evolutionary institutional change by a process that John R. Commons called *artificial selection*. In contrast to biological systems with their "natural" selection, the evolutionary change in human systems is purposeful and instrumental. It is motivated, *ab initio*, by an emerging consensus concerning some persistent problematic situation requiring correction. Notice that this is not an exercise in creating a clear and direct mapping between a single *a priori* end state and the evolutionary trajectory of the constructed institutional architecture that will—it is expected—produce (result in) that end state. Evolutionary institutional change is the process of creating—by collective action in the legislature, the courts, and various administrative agencies—new legal parameters of the national economy. Commons coined the term artificial selection to emphasize that it is a process of individuals (citizens) and authoritative agents (legislators, judges, administrative officials) "looking to the future" and trying to figure out how that future ought to unfold. While biological systems are understood in terms of their function, human systems are understood in terms of their evolving purposes (Bromley 2006).

Do development experts, whether officials in a particular country or international experts, understand those purposes? Do they know how to think of them in evolutionary terms?

We start by acknowledging that human systems, just as with natural systems, are always coming from something rather than going towards something. By this we mean that there is no higher purpose or desired end state for either natural systems or human systems. Natural systems evolve by accidents of variation and selection. Human systems evolve by a purposeful and continual process that is animated by the constant need to solve new and quite unexpected problems. The teleology of human systems cannot be considered in terms of some meta-goal (or meta-purpose). Rather, the pertinent teleology of human systems is of a rather more practical kind. It is one in which societies continually modify the institutional architecture so that the new problematic circumstances might be overcome. With this in mind we can see that an evolutionary theory of economic change—or an economic theory that is evolutionary—requires four components.

First, if we are to understand human systems in evolutionary terms we must find some source of *animation* in virtue of which a nation's institutional structure comes to be seen as plausibly ill-suited to the realization of some desired circumstances in the future. Think of this as the gradual accumulation of plausible reasons to question the *status quo ante* institutional setup. Perhaps rural unemployment is high and seems resistant to the standard policy prescriptions to bring it down. Perhaps problems in biodiversity protection reveal defects in protocols for sustainable use of important natural habitats. Perhaps urban water systems are not performing as expected. Perhaps squatters have taken over vacant urban land against the wishes of the government. Perhaps agricultural chemicals are causing destruction of artisanal fisheries. Perhaps soil erosion is severe and undermining the key asset of poor farmers. Perhaps irrigation systems have fallen into disrepair.

SELECTION—NATURAL VS. ARTIFICIAL

Human systems are arenas of artificial selection. Humans are best considered as clever animals—we are superb diagnosticians. When confronted by surprise we first look for reasons that might explain that unwanted surprise. When we believe we have identified the reasons for the surprise we then go to work on those reasons. Can we alter those reasons in some way to rectify the unwanted surprise?

We write our own future as we come to grips with unwanted surprise. We are pragmatic instrumentalists. Commons called this "artificial selection" to distinguish it from the process of passive selection in the natural world. Humans are not passive recipients of the changes going on around us. Rather, we observe them, judge them in terms of our own vision of what we think we desire, and if we find them lacking in redeeming value we actively seek to modify them.

The problems of such urgent concern must be seen as the plausible entailments—the quite expected implications—of institutional arrangements that are no longer suited to new circumstances in the economy. That is, these problematic outcomes arise not because of "market failure" (or flawed prices), but because they are the result of newly inappropriate institutional arrangements that constitute the causal structure of plausibly perverse incentives. These flawed incentives then induce unwanted individual behaviors. The correction of these unwanted outcomes will require some institutional changes. This first stage in institutional innovation is therefore the emerging recognition of a problematic situation requiring deeper investigation. The problems are irritants to the "body politic."

Second, once it is acknowledged that existing outcomes are no longer desired, an evolutionary economics suggests the need for a focused *diagnostic* phase in which the plausible reasons for the existing problem are carefully worked out. Why, exactly, is the current problem occurring? What are the causes or reasons for this problem? We may think of this aspect as a quest for the specific reasons why particular institutional arrangements are plausibly implicated in the problematic situation now requiring correction. This diagnostic activity brings focused and concerted effort to the acquisition of an understanding as to why, exactly, the current institutional setup—and its attendant incentive structure—is producing these unwanted outcomes. This diagnostic step is essential if governments and their donor partners are to be successful in identifying what must be done to correct the individual economizing behaviors that now seem to be responsible for the perceived problematic outcomes.

Third, an evolutionary approach requires a process of *adjustment* in the institutional arrangements plausibly implicated as the reasons for the problematic outcomes.

It is here that legislators, administrative officials, judges, and other authoritative agents must become involved in the gradual process of modifying the pertinent institutional arrangements that are now acknowledged to be the source of the problem—and thus in need of revision.

This essential process of adjustment in the institutional setup of an economy will require several things. First, there must be an explanation as to the reasons for the newly recognized problematic situation. Second, one or more policy options—think of them as policy prescriptions—that seem likely to deliver improved outcomes in the future must be identified. Third, there must be general acceptance of the implied predictions that if one or more of the policy prescriptions is adopted then the currently unwanted outcomes will be corrected and the situation can reasonably be expected to improve in specific ways. This third step entails the actual formulation (design) of new institutions (new rules). At this point we encounter the forward-looking activity in which particular institutional arrangements in the economy are re-designed with the explicit intent of bringing about more preferred outcomes.

Finally, there must be a *stopping rule* in this process of institutional adjustment. This stopping rule represents the result of the collective working out of reasons to adopt a particular new institutional arrangement over other plausible alternatives—including the existing institutional setup. It is here that participants in the process of institutional adjustment reach an agreement that some new particular variation on the *status quo ante* institutional setup seems like the best thing to do at this time. This emerging agreement is an implicit ratification of the need for institutional change, the specifics of the preferred institutional change that is called for, and the need to let the specific institutional change get underway so that the results can be observed and evaluated. The stopping rule in an evolutionary system must provide sufficient reasons to act in particular ways, and then to allow the new institutional setup to give rise to new patterns of interaction—and new outcomes. Have we really corrected the problem of rural unemployment? Have we adequately fixed the prior flaws in sustainable use of biodiversity? Can it be claimed that the performance of urban water systems has really improved? Has the destruction of artisanal fisheries been halted? Is soil erosion really less severe than it was previously? This final aspect concerns *adaptation*.

Notice that adaptation need not imply that the problem has been fixed once and for all. Perhaps the imagined solution to a problem is not quite right because the original problem had not been correctly diagnosed. Or, if the diagnosis was correct, perhaps the institutional change introduced to fix the problem was not quite right. Perhaps the specific contexts changed. Perhaps other institutional change was underway at the same time. The matter will be revisited and a new solution will be advanced.

Finding reasons for reform

The primary challenge in policy reform—institutional change—is to recognize that public policies in an economy are not mere "disembodied" rules derived from abstract principles of economic efficiency or political expediency. Public policies are the codification of evolving principles of socially approved behavior. A policy (a rule) requiring children to remain in school until a certain age is not just an arbitrary exercises of state power over children and their parents. Such rules (policies) evolve over time as societies collectively reflect on changing views about child labor and the importance of education. Pollution-control policies are yet another illustration of changing social beliefs. At one time rivers were for transportation and the disposal of human and industrial waste. Gradually the social purpose of rivers underwent change, and with those evolving ideas about what rivers are for, new policies were adopted to change how humans interacted with rivers.

The institutional architecture of nation-states is therefore a reflection of underlying customs and norms that are anchored in the past, yet gradually changing to embody new scarcities, new technological opportunities and threats, new attitudes about how society ought to be organized, and new priorities that now seem urgent. Notice here the profound role of customary practices mediated by the necessity to keep an economy "becoming." That customary behavior is predicated on accepted norms and codified laws, and such behavior serves to reinforce the legitimacy of the habits and rules (policies) upon which such behavior rests. Human practices give rise to rules about those practices which then serve to legitimize those very practices.

To return to the example of pollution, the custom of depositing human and industrial waste in nearby rivers emerged from the belief that this is precisely what rivers are for. With this belief in hand it was obvious enough that a new rule (a new pollution policy) to prevent pollution would not be the sensible thing to do. We see that a new policy on pollution of rivers would be quite impossible until widely shared beliefs about the purpose of rivers had undergone a profound shift. In this case, the process of policy reform was not really about whether pollution is good or bad (or right or wrong). The social discussion—the political debate—concerned the purpose of rivers. As long as rivers carry away pollutants at no obvious cost to the polluter, and until opponents could create a new vision concerning the purpose of rivers, it would be foolish (economically irrational) to insist that pollution be stopped. Once it was documented that pollution killed fish and other living creatures, and that pollution made rivers unsafe for swimming, rivers acquired a new purpose. Only then was it possible to introduce new policies to prohibit pollution. Policy reforms must be anchored on the emergence of new beliefs about what now seems the better thing to do (Bromley 2006).

We can add structure to the foregoing by drawing attention to Figure 5.1. Here we show three broad "realms" in society—a realm in which ideas and beliefs are debated, a realm in which the policies (laws) of the economy are formulated, and a realm in which people go about their daily lives as workers, owners, and consumers. We have, therefore, realms of: (1) beliefs; (2) policies; and (3) actions.

In the left-hand box in Figure 5.1 we see "people doing" and thereby producing particular social outcomes—child labor, pollution of rivers, plantation agriculture, bribery along major highways. It is here, in the realm of actions and their inevitable outcomes (see Figure 2.1), that certain aspects of the economy will come to be

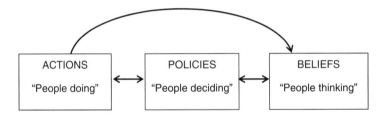

FIGURE 5.1 Realms of actions, policies, and beliefs

considered defective. It is here that the early interest in altering behaviors will be focused—polluters must stop, children must be in school.

But of course in democratic societies we do not simply order individuals to stop polluting or to put their children in school. These behavioral changes need to be discussed, evaluated, and debated. Commissions need to be created, the evidence needs to be marshaled, and reasons need to be advanced.

These deliberative processes occur in the realm of beliefs (right-hand box). It is here that people find their customary beliefs challenged by others with different beliefs. Change is rarely quick, nor straightforward. New beliefs must run the gauntlet of hostile challenges by those well served by the *status quo ante*. Those advocating new beliefs will be labeled trouble-makers. Those defending current policies will be called different names. Eventually a new set of beliefs will coalesce and this brings us to the middle box in Figure 5.1. This is the purpose of parliaments. Here a new institutional architecture will be created. Policy reform happens here.

To return to an earlier theme, notice that once these new policies are in place, and people's actions become accommodated to the new rules, their altered behavior will—in the fullness of time—come to be seen as normal, rational, and correct. It will soon be said: "How is it possible that we once allowed child labor?" Or, "I cannot imagine that chemical factories were once able to dispose of their poisonous wastes in this river."

The point here is that customary individual behaviors always change in response to new institutional arrangements that modify the structure of economic sanctions and incentives.

Institutional change is a process of "cycling through" the three realms depicted in Figure 5.1. New beliefs—animated by unwanted outcomes in, or emanating from, the left box—are worked out until a "better idea" emerges in the realm of beliefs. Once that better idea has been accepted, the policy process results in new institutional arrangements (rules) that will redefine the fields of action for those "people doing" in the left box. The economy becomes by a continual process of re-creating the institutional arrangements (middle box) that redefine fields of action for individuals in the left box. New beliefs inform and rationalize new rules that allow and restrain individual behaviors. Those new behaviors produce outcomes that will be judged good or bad, and those assessments will then signal to the realm of beliefs that things are now "fixed" or that yet further manipulation is called for. The economy becomes.

Policy reform as informed problem solving

Our approach to the problems of vulnerable people and vulnerable states, with its roots in pragmatism, is a diagnostic endeavor (Bromley 2006). There is obvious relevance to an approach that is concerned with understanding the causes of—and the reasons for—particular social and economic problems. The general approach is concerned with policy diagnostics. At the core of our approach is an epistemology—a way of knowing—called the *method of hypothesis*. Aristotle called this approach "diagnosis." Some philosophers of science call it "inference to the best explanation." Charles Sanders Peirce, the founder of pragmatism, called it "abduction," and one of the founders of institutional economics, John R. Commons, adopted the abductive syllogism as an essential method for diagnosing problems. Peirce insisted that the human mind is animated by the irritation of doubt. Specifically, "the action of thought is excited by the irritation of doubt, and ceases when belief is attained; so that the production of belief is the sole function of thought" (Peirce 1957: 36).

What Peirce had in mind here is that our first instinct as humans is to confront the unsettling reaction to sudden doubt and surprise. The pertinence of abduction (diagnostics) to development assistance should be obvious. Why are rice yields so meager? Why is there such a poor record of job creation in this economy? Why won't farmers adopt modern seeds? Why don't local entrepreneurs make better use of credit? Why are fertilizer supplies always so uncertain? Why don't credit markets work better? Why are timber harvesters given free rein in the forests? Why doesn't the government take more aggressive measures to prevent destruction of biodiversity? Why is groundwater being extracted at rates in excess of recharge? Why don't irrigators form organizations and rules to mediate water allocation? Why are industrial firms allowed to discharge toxic wastes directly into rivers? Why are there such large subsidies on particular agricultural crops?

These questions—and many more—animate thought about development problems and about the relative efficacy of particular institutional changes (policy reform) to fix those problems. Notice that different disciplines—different "knowledge communities"—will offer competing reasons (hypotheses) for these observed development problems. Economists will diagnose these problems in one way, while anthropologists or sociologists will diagnose these problems in slightly different ways. The point is obvious, but still worthy of emphasis. If we do not develop clear and coherent definitions of the *development problem* then it is quite unlikely that programmatic initiatives to correct those problems will be pertinent or successful. It should also be apparent that if the "development problem" is not well specified and agreed upon, it will be impossible to determine whether or not development activities have been successful (Riddell 2007).

Implications

There is a danger that some of the deductive truths of economics as it is taught these days create impatience for reflections on what people believe, and how they come to believe it. Preferences are assumed to be given and stable, motivations are clear and centered on maximizing wellbeing, and the central task of development assistance is to figure out how to let these truths do good work in the service of economic growth. Countries merely need to wise up and introduce efficient institutions. The past several decades have found these verities embodied in the inductive deceit known as the Washington Consensus—rich countries have these particular institutions, you should have them too (and then you too will be rich).

It is our central proposition that the international development enterprise is now foundering because of this misplaced confidence, and because of the inability to find new ways to think about the development challenge. Diagnosis must now supplant *a priori* convictions.

6
THE DIAGNOSTIC IMPERATIVE

By induction, we conclude that facts similar to observed facts are true in cases not examined. By hypothesis [diagnosis or abduction], we conclude the existence of a fact quite different from anything observed, from which, according to known laws, something observed would necessarily result. The former is reasoning from particulars to the general law; the latter from effect to cause. The former classifies, the latter explains.

(Peirce 1957: 136)

Setting the stage

The manifold vulnerabilities that afflict Kweku Owiredu of Ghana—and millions like him throughout the developing world—must be understood as symptoms of more fundamental problems. Why can't he get fertilizer on time? Why are the police and customs officials always seeking bribes? Why is it impossible to get extension advice? Why is electricity unavailable when he needs it most? Why doesn't the surface irrigation system work? Why is it impossible to get agricultural credit at any price? Why is the cement factory able to pollute his fields and thereby destroy his beautiful tomatoes? Why is there no one to whom he can turn for solutions to these impediments? Why must it be like this?

In Chapter 4 we introduced *abduction* as the essential diagnostic epistemology that remains too rare in most development assistance programs. We now elaborate on that idea by making reference to the plight of Mr. Owiredu.

The surprising fact $\underline{C}$ is observed.
If $\underline{A}$ were true then $\underline{C}$ would be expected (and therefore not surprising).
Since $\underline{C}$ is indeed observed, $\underline{A}$ must be true.

In the above abductive syllogism, the surprising fact $\underline{C}$ is the inability of Mr. Owiredu to obtain practical solutions to his many problems—such problems standing as the reasons for his vulnerability. In addressing this surprise, the diagnostic imperative would compel the development analyst to formulate a set of sequenced hypotheses— $\underline{A}$ in the above syllogism—which provide the explanation (the reasons) for Mr. Owiredu's inability.[1] Once the constituents of $\underline{A}$ have been determined, development programs could be crafted to address them in a step-wise process so that the most important binding constraint is rectified first, then the next binding constraint is addressed, and so-on down the list (the series) of constraints.

We stress the importance of ranking the constituents of $\underline{A}$ in the order in which they must be confronted and, with the benefit of appropriate policy reforms, rectified. It does little good to present governments with an undifferentiated (non-prioritized) list of 10–12 complex and difficult actions to be taken, without at the same time giving them advice (and reasons) why some must be undertaken first, second, and third, while the others can be addressed in a future program. Governments do not have unlimited budgets for reform, and they have other pressing needs to be addressed. Most important, policy reform consumes a great deal of political capital and government officials must be aware of the costs and benefits of using that capital. Governments, as with business entrepreneurs, must be cautiously opportunistic.

Notice the emphasis here on diagnosis, explanation, and reason giving. The emphasis on reason giving is important because decision makers—and the general public—will often focus inordinate attention on the surprise ($\underline{C}$) rather than on the plausible reasons for that surprise. A diagnostic approach properly focuses attention on the constituents of $\underline{A}$. Doing so will reveal that many of the constituents of $\underline{A}$ (credit rationing, bribes and delays, the absence of laws on pollution) are themselves the surprising results of yet prior reasons ($\underline{A}'$) in the causal chain. The constituents of $\underline{A}'$ then stand implicated as the plausible reasons for $\underline{A}$. Candidate constituents of $\underline{A}'$ might be: (1) political control of the banking system causing it to favor the export sector over domestic agriculture; (2) corrupt police officials and perhaps the Minister of Security; and (3) political clout of the owner of the cement factory.

A comprehensive diagnostic approach offers the only route to plausible explanations for flawed social and economic outcomes that constitute the reasons for individual and household vulnerability. With those explanations (reasons) in hand, the development official can focus attention on working with governments to undertake the necessary policy reforms. The resulting (new) institutional arrangements—and associated organizational changes—will comprise the essential policy reforms that are expected to bring about an improved constellation of outcomes for farmers such as Mr. Owiredu. The process of policy reform requires a comprehensive understanding of the relation between certain observed problematic situations (what we call unwanted social outcomes), and the underlying reasons—explanations—for those unwanted settings and circumstances.

It is much too common to blame these unwanted outcomes on perverse behaviors—most often "risk aversion"—on the part of farmers. These rather standard psychological accounts are impertinent precisely because they overlook the fact that individuals often have no choices to make. If you cannot move, you are not choosing to stand still. In such cases, there is no deep psychological motive (risk aversion) on display. There is, instead, a deliberate, and quite rational response to a situation that the farmer has observed and assessed over a long period of time. As a Bayesian learner, the farmer knows very well that he has no choices to make. For risk aversion to serve as a reason (an explanation) for observed inaction there must be a feasible set of choices over which choice can be exercised. In our setting near Kumasi, no options are available. Vulnerability concerns the comprehensive absence of choice.

The diagnostic imperative provides improved understanding of particular behaviors and correlated outcomes through deployment of a structured search for underlying reasons. Our approach to creating economic coherence is predicated on the view that those reasons are to be found in the institutional arrangements that define (specify) the decision space—the field of action—for individual farmers, traders, commercial businesses, police, customs officials, and agricultural lenders. Prevailing institutional arrangements offer pathways to explanation precisely because these institutions parameterize individual domains of choice. Institutions comprise the rules for human action, and therefore institutions are instrumental to observed outcomes. It is common to regard prices as decisive for human action. But it is essential to recall that all prices in a market economy are themselves the product of underlying institutional arrangements. If gasoline is taxed heavily, the "demand" for gasoline at the pump will differ profoundly from what it would be if there were no taxes levied on gasoline. Prices matter, but prices do not just magically appear—they are products of the institutional architecture of an economy.[2] Getting prices "right" means first bringing about institutional change.

The diagnostic imperative reveals two salient lessons for policy reform. First, unwanted social and economic outcomes never arise for just one reason. The obvious implication is that undesired outcomes can only be understood—explained—if the analyst establishes a suite of reasons for those outcomes. Second, it is insufficient to stop diagnostic work at the first sign of a plausible cause or reason for the problematic result. The analyst must go beyond the first appearance of responsibility for the results, and then keep working back to find the underlying prior conditions that seem to lie behind the plausible explanation. We must look for $\underline{A}'$, and then $\underline{A}''$, and perhaps even $\underline{A}'''$.

In other words, if we suppose that we have explained (as opposed to justifying) behavior when we find that it is consistent with a particular piece of theory then we have acquired belief of a very meager kind. More importantly, we have terminated our inquiries precisely where they will soon start to pay large explanatory dividends. Premature claims of victory are only part of the problem. The flaw of confirmationism is compounded by the belief that economic phenomena can be fully understood by reference to independent variables that are themselves strictly economic in character. Any effort to explain economic phenomena by reference only to economic phenomena introduces a fatal circularity into economic work. To quote Joseph Schumpeter:

> …when we succeed in finding a definite causal relation between two phenomena, our problem is solved if the one which plays the "causal" role is non-economic. We have then accomplished what we, as economists, are capable of in the case in question and we must give place to other disciplines. If, on the other hand, the causal factor is itself economic in nature, we must continue our explanatory efforts until we ground upon a non-economic bottom.
>
> *(Schumpeter 1961: 4–5)*

The point here is simple: one has not explained economic phenomena—and institutional arrangements are the essence of economic phenomena—until one encounters one or more non-economic independent variables (Bromley 2006: 69–70).

The essential distinction between reasons and causes

The quest to diagnose unwanted social and economic outcomes that bear down on vulnerable people and vulnerable states must be understood as a *process of inference*. When inference is underway, the development expert is leveraging a few things we think we believe into a clearer picture of a few troublesome things that we wish to understand. This focus on inference reinforces the point that diagnostics cannot be concerned with mere analysis. Rather, diagnosis must concern explanation. While the term "analytical" is usually presented as an activity of great importance—and as a favorable adjective to deploy in scientific writing and speaking—analysis is a mere dress rehearsal for explanation.

To *analyze* a specific phenomenon or event is to seek a pattern of relations among several other seemingly pertinent phenomena. The focus of analysis concerns *how* something works as it does. By way of contrast, to *explain* a specific phenomenon or event is to find the exact circumstances without which the specific phenomenon of interest would be quite impossible. The focus of explanation concerns *why* something happens. And when we turn our attention to explanation, it is necessary to distinguish between causes and reasons.

A cause is an external entity from which the change (or the ending of the change) first starts. John presses a switch, and thereby causes the light to come on. Pressing the switch is called the mechanical—the proximate—cause of the light coming on. But why did John press the switch? What can explain this new circumstance? John did not press the switch without a reason. Of course John's reasons have something to do with changing the light in the room. John envisions a "lighter future" by pressing the switch. The cause of the light is an act of pressing the switch. The reason for the light is a desire to eliminate the unwelcome darkness in the room. Reasons concern outcomes in the future. Philosophers call such purposeful actions "final causes." That is, "the final cause of an occurrence is an event in the future for the sake of which the occurrence takes place...things are explained by the purposes they serve" (Russell 1945: 67). We see that a reason is that for the sake of which an action is taken—the purpose the action is to serve.

Causes, on the other hand, are antecedent conditions that necessarily (and sufficiently) produce subsequent phenomena. Causes explain the future in terms of actions taken in the present—pressing the light switch will light the room. Reasons are purposeful and intentioned actions that are leveraged by outcomes in the future. Reasons explain actions taken now in terms of expected outcomes in the future. If you want more light in the room, press that switch. The purpose of reasoning is to form inferences about something unknown but of interest to us. In diagnostic work, the reason we reason is to find reasons for events that seem unreasonable. When confronted with surprising and unwanted social and economic outcomes, the analyst must find reasons for those outcomes. It will not do to settle for mere causes.

We now turn to several examples of the institutional bases for unwanted social outcomes. Our intent is to demonstrate the practical value of comprehensive diagnostics.

The instrumental nature of institutions

We here demonstrate the instrumental nature of the relation between existing institutional arrangements and the persistence of unwanted outcomes. In each instance discussed below, individuals and households suffer serious vulnerabilities arising from perverse institutional arrangements. When the development community understands the causal relation between existing institutions and particular unwanted outcomes, it is then possible to demonstrate how careful policy diagnostics will provide the causal basis for targeted policy reform. The preferred term these days is "evidence-based" reforms. The resulting policy reform will then constitute the institutional innovation necessary for rectifying the persistent unwanted social outcomes. That is, modifying existing institutional arrangements—altering individual choice sets—will redirect individual behaviors. *Policy reform* is the name of the process whereby purposeful institutional change brings forth new more desired outcomes.

The specific examples to be discussed here concern: (1) pollution; (2) the destruction of biodiversity; (3) dysfunctional irrigation systems; (4) the resource curse; and (5) attenuated agricultural markets.

Pollution as cost shifting

Our Ghanaian farmer is the obvious victim of cost shifting, and his exposure to unwanted costs is an illustration of the many social and economic problems traceable to perversely flawed institutional arrangements. The basic problem here is that the cement factory is able to shift costs to others in an example of what we call *externalities*. Externalities are present when some of the costs (or benefits) of a particular economic activity fall on individuals and firms outside of (external to) the decision processes of individual firms. Here is an example of how the prevailing institutional structure is permissive of cost shifting because, as in Table 4.1, the cement factory stands in a legal situation of privilege while others—those harmed by the shifting of costs—are defined by a legal setting of no right against this shifting of costs on to them. In practical terms, this means that if Mr. Owiredu would go to the Ghanaian courts in hopes of forcing the cement factory to stop damaging his tomatoes, he would be told: "Sorry, you have no right to stop the pollution—you must go to the parliament if you expect the courts to enforce your interests against the pollution damages you now suffer." Courts do not pass legislation—they interpret what legislatures have passed. Here there is no law against pollution.

In Figure 6.1 we depict the production of cement in the vicinity of Mr. Owiredu's farm. Notice in the lower panel that the technology of cement production implies the generation of costs beyond the decision space of the cement factory. It is this element that holds serious implications for Mr. Owiredu and his neighbors.

As above, the current legal setting—the existing institutional arrangement—is permissive of pollution by the cement factory which means that it stands in a legal position of privilege while the victims of pollution have no right. Under this institutional regime we see that the result would be the generation of the quantity of

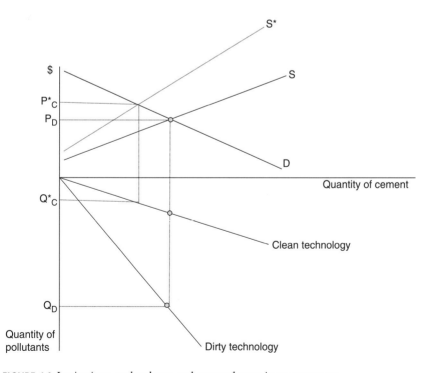

FIGURE 6.1 Institutions, technology, and external costs in an economy

pollutants Q_D per unit of time. The inference here is that "clean" technology—devices to trap and dispose of the abundant dust—is more expensive for the cement factory to use than continuing to use its existing "dirty" technology. If the law is permissive in this regard, firms will seek to shift pollution costs on to others rather than to pay the higher price for the preventive devices. However, if the legal regime would change to give victims of pollution a right to be free of these unwanted external (shifted) costs, polluters such as the cement factory harming Mr. Owiredu would suddenly find themselves with a duty not to pollute. Under this new institutional setup, consider the modifications in Figure 6.1.

Specifically, the legal change could require the installation of dust-trapping devices (clean technology), or it would insist that the factory stop operating. Notice that this institutional change would increase the costs of cement in the Ghanaian market—a desired outcome since, in light of the current externalities, cement production does not take full account of its associated social costs. Cement is too cheap. In comparative-statics terms, the expenditure for the new "scrubbers" would shift the supply curve of cement production upward to S* leading to a new equilibrium price at P^*_C, a lower production of cement, and an eventual reduction in the generation of pollutants from the original Q_D to the new Q^*_C.

Alternatively, policy reform leading to a new legal regime of duty for polluters and rights for the victims of pollution could take a different form. Specifically, rather than a mandate on technology, the new institutional setup could impose a pollution fee on the damages produced by the emission of pollutants. We call this fee a Pigovian tax (after A.C. Pigou who first identified the concept of marginal damages). We can use Figure 6.2 to illustrate the adjustment process from this policy reform.

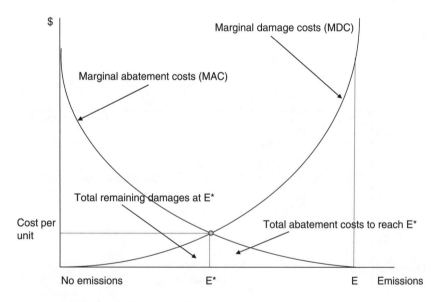

FIGURE 6.2 Pollution damages and the optimal Pigovian tax

Recall that the status-quo institutional setup is one of privilege for polluters and no right for the victims of pollution. This starting point would put us at the far right of Figure 6.2 (point E). The curve labeled MDC (marginal damage costs) depicts the increase in pollution damages as emissions increase from zero at the far left of the figure to their current high level at E. As we know from the calculus, the area under a marginal damage curve represents total pollution damages from emissions at E. Assume that these damages traced out by MDC are the result of pollution from a single cement factory harming a small number of vegetable farmers. We can then understand the MDC curve as tracing out necessary expenditures by the farmers to prevent cement dust harming their tomatoes. Perhaps they must construct plastic shields over their fields, and perhaps add large fans to blow the harmful dust away.

Notice the second curve in Figure 6.2—marginal abatement costs (MAC). This curve depicts the necessary costs that would be paid by the polluter (the cement factory) should it be required to clean up (abate) its emissions of cement dust that now go directly into the atmosphere. The status quo point in the diagram (E) is a classic example of the polluting firm saving on pollution abatement cost by discharging its wastes into the atmosphere. Recall that pollution is an example of cost shifting by the polluter. We see here that the polluter is shifting costs to the nearby farmers.

The Pigovian tax on damages would force the cement factory to pay a fee that traced out the path of the MDC curve moving from right to left until pollution is reduced far below its current level at E. Notice that these costs traced out by the curve of marginal damages would exactly meet the necessary expenditures by the farmers to prevent damage by the dust. Indeed the curve MDC can be thought of as the demand curve for clean air by the farmers. This curve traces out the marginal benefits to the farmers of clean air—and it is a benefit since it depicts the marginal value of clean air.

Notice that at the far right of the figure the polluting firm is faced with two choices—it can pay the marginal abatement costs (MAC) to clean its own dusty discharge, or it can pay the farmers the magnitude of damages (this would be the Pigovian tax). Because MAC initially lies very much below MDC it is obvious that the cement factory will decide that cleaning up its own wastes is much more cost-effective than paying the farmers to correct the pollution as it arrives at their fields. Notice the macroeconomic wisdom of this approach—overall economic efficiency is served by having the polluting firm clean up its own mess rather than shifting those costs to the victim. There is also a sense of justice in this approach.

When emissions are reduced to E^* an important threshold is reached. Here the marginal cost to the polluting firm of cleaning up its own emissions (MAC) is equal to the marginal cost of having the victim do so (MDC). This new level of emissions (E^*) is an economically defensible outcome because any movement away from E^* entails inefficiency. To the left of E^* the polluter is paying more to rectify pollutants than the damages that would result from that reduced level of pollution (shown by the MDC curve). To the right of E^* the damages inflicted on the farmers (MDC) are in excess of what it would cost the polluter to correct the situation (MAC).

Policy reform—institutional change—creates a new structure of rights and duties regarding the shifting of costs from one party to another. It is a common mistake to assume that the first option above—the requirement to clean up pollution by installing devices to capture cement dust—is an example of "command and control" while the second option is an example of "letting the market work." This is mistaken because both policy options are examples of policy reform that alters the institutional structure—the legal parameters—of the economy. The political message must first be clear that pollution is no longer tolerated. We saw in Chapter 5 that new beliefs about pollution motivate the adoption of new institutions about pollution, that then yield new individual behavior with respect to pollution, and this then leads to less harm being visited on former victims of pollution.

Protecting ecosystems and ecosystem services

There is widespread support for programs that pay (or reward) local people to develop sustainable management protocols for particular ecosystem services. The difficulty to be encountered in policy reform in this area arises from what we call *incentive compatibility*. Incentive-compatible institutional arrangements are those in which participants in a particular situation defined by those institutions know they will maximize their well-being if and only if they respond honestly to any information request inherent in—implied by—the specific situation. For the design of programs to reward individuals for the provision of ecosystem services, incentive compatibility requires that the new policy setting be one that each participant will honestly reveal to the creator of the new institutional arrangements—think of this as a quasi-"auctioneer"—the exact minimum necessary to alter that individual's behavior so that this new behavior aligns perfectly with the desires of the auctioneer whose job is to accomplish the purposes of the program.

In correctly designed programs, the auctioneer obtains exactly what she seeks, she pays the absolute minimum necessary to bring about the desired behavioral change, and she knows that she can trust the individual whose behavior she seeks to modify. In most instances, a payment level is set knowing that some local participants will receive payments in excess of what is required to purchase their compliance, while other participants will receive payments that are less than necessary to purchase their full compliance (and they perform in an indifferent manner), and some individuals or communities choose not to participate at all—and so receive nothing.

The central problem with such schemes is that they are difficult to implement and sustain because they operate in a realm of unequal information, and of unequal power—a superior and an inferior. Familiar terms that describe these games include parent–child, boss–worker, and donor–recipient. The first person in these dualities is called the principal and the second person is called the agent. We call these principal–agent games. The challenge in such games is to get the agent to do what the principal wants, and to make sure that the agent is induced to be honest in her revelations about what she is doing—and what she promises to do when the principal is not there to observe her behavior. The challenge for the principal is to pay no more than is absolutely necessary in order to induce the agent to behave as desired. The assumption here is that the principal knows the precise willingness to pay to achieve particular outcomes and wishes, therefore, to "purchase" compliance—or specific environmental services—for less than that magnitude. Clearly good information plays a key role here—each side negotiates more effectively if they understand their own reservation price and have some sense of the willingness to pay—or the willingness to supply—of the other party. For example, principals will often know the likely costs of an alternative management regime before negotiating a payment. On the other hand, agents may have a better idea of other program aspects. All such programs function in a realm of asymmetric information.

In addition to this disparity in information, unequal power arises because individuals from outside of a particular community offer financial inducements to alter the habituated behavior of individuals inside of particular communities. Those coming from the outside are able to take their financial offer to a large number of potential recipients, but those out on the ground often must accept what is on offer or receive nothing at all. And of course the poorer they are the more eager they will be to accept an offer—the poor can be counted on to sell out cheaply. In economic terms, the poor have a low reservation price. Their very vulnerability puts them in a weak bargaining position.

We alluded above to habituated behavior. This idea is important because when outsiders look in on a community there is a presumption that each day the behavior on display is the result of constant calculation of gains and losses across a wide number of margins. This presumption would be mistaken. Human behavior is seriously habituated on the basis of long experience with what seems to work. Only when confronted by surprise do individuals stop and reassess what they are doing— and why they are doing it. This matter of deep habituation is relevant in the current context if we suppose that individuals out on the ground—embedded in communities defined by habituated behavior—can be easily dislodged from a lifetime of choices with respect to their natural surroundings that are suddenly of such abiding interest to us from the outside, and most assuredly taken for granted by those who are embedded therein.

The above comments may seem surprising in a realm that is often characterized as "win–win"—that property in which both sides get what it is they think they want. Unfortunately, it is too easy to imagine that outsiders can get what they want, and local people can get what they want. Yet these assured gains are only possible if the arrangement is sustainable. The sustainability of such programs requires that the very greatest attention be paid to incentive design that acknowledges the environmental status quo against which progress is to be measured. The fundamental question becomes: Are individuals being rewarded for correcting that which they have previously harmed, or to preclude them doing similar—or different—harms in the future? We can think of this as a problem of defining the *reference level* (Bromley and Hodge 1990). In particular, what, exactly, is the ecological status quo against which change is to be judged?

This issue is directly relevant to problems faced by the Global Environment Facility (GEF). The GEF has struggled with the conceptual and empirical problem of *incremental costs and benefits* (also referred to as "additionality"). The GEF wishes to induce particular behaviors that would not be part of regular project and program design. But with learning, and with associated behavioral change, it becomes difficult to identify truly incremental behavior. As concern for nature becomes more completely embedded in program and project design—think of it as "mainstreaming"—the actual incremental portion will diminish. And that is good because it means that improved environmental behaviors and outcomes will occur without the need to keep paying for those behaviors and outcomes.

But there is an alternative scenario. While payments for certain behaviors with respect to nature may succeed in altering particular behaviors with respect to nature, if the payments gradually disappear there is a good chance that the desired behaviors will revert to their former state. Once the principal stops paying for particular behaviors, the agent has good reasons to assume that the newly adopted behaviors are no longer desired. And if those behaviors are no longer financially rewarding we should not be surprised if those behaviors change. New habituated behaviors cannot emerge quickly. And therefore when payments stop, behavior reverts to its old norm.

Program sustainability can be improved by paying special attention to the nature of the policy instruments employed. There is a continuum of policy approaches to encourage local communities to protect and enhance biodiversity. We call these: (1) facilitative policies; (2) inducing policies; and (3) injunctive policies. Each instrument choice holds different implications for the sustainability of these programs.

Facilitative policies

Facilitative policies allow individuals to undertake behavioral changes that are consistent with the long-run interests of both the principal and the agent, but not in the short-run interest of the agent. For instance, there can be a range of behavioral changes that agents might like to pursue, said changes being coincident with changes that the principal wishes for, but particular barriers stand in the way of implementing those changes. We can think of these as hurdle problems. They are hurdle problems because a small amount of financial assistance, of limited duration, can produce lasting benefits to both the principal and the agent. For instance, short-term liquidity problems might be rectified and from then on the agent would be quite willing and able to persist on a new behavioral trajectory.

Perhaps a few small check-dams will stabilize stream banks and allow for the production of freshwater fish to supplement local protein supplies. Other small investments might permit a trajectory of future behaviors that will have desired ecological attributes. The inducements do not always need to be in terms of cash. Perhaps limited opportunities for subsidized credit will be sufficient.

The opportunity to undertake facilitative policies is a reminder that we must always initiate the diagnosis of particular problems with an assessment of the livelihoods of those whose behavior we seek to alter. There are a number of actions taken by local people that they know are not in their long-run interest. Unfortunately, many of them are locked into certain patterns of interaction by their inability to deal with the hurdle problem. Proper diagnosis requires a search for the real reasons why they are doing what they are doing. Once that is understood, it will be possible to formulate facilitative policies that have reassuring livelihood implications, and good environmental implications.

Inducing policies

Inducing policies realign incentives for those settings and circumstances in which the long-run interests of the principal and the agent do not converge. Note that unlike facilitative policies, where the long-run interests of the principal and the agent are coincidental, here one needs policies to address the divergence in the interests of the principal and the agent. There is no hurdle problem here because of a divergence in the desired long-run behavioral trajectory. Behavioral changes cannot be facilitated—they must be induced.

It is here that incentive sustainability becomes a serious challenge for the simple reason that financial inducements are rarely sufficient to alter long-run behaviors. This is so because the economic and ecological circumstances of a group of people are always in the process of becoming. It is impossible to design incentive-compatible institutions (rules and incentives) that will do the necessary work into the future because neither the principal nor the agents know precisely what the future will bring. The challenge for efficient institutional design, in the form of required payments that will bring about specific environmental behaviors, is daunting. We are reminded of this challenge in the recent dramatic changes in grain prices driven by the frenzy over bio-fuels. Land previously set aside in conservation reserves, in wildlife areas, and land devoted to forage crops, was rapidly converted to grain production. And soil erosion from land devoted to grains is higher than if that same land were to remain in its current uses. We see that it is difficult, if not impossible, to design payment schemes for ecologically benign behaviors in the face of such unforeseen economic circumstances.

This reminds us that inducing policies, if they are to give rise to sustainable ecological benefits, must constantly be updated and modified. Notice that this locks the principal and the agent into a continual game of re-negotiation. Those out on the ground, who may not immediately be charmed at being treated as the agent of someone else, will not find this a compelling prospect. The more dynamic is the co-evolution of the economic and the natural systems in a particular location, the more difficult will be the challenge of instrument design—and the more fragile will be the ongoing relationship between those who seek to alter behavior, and those who will soon come to see themselves as mere objects in the increasingly vexing challenge of keeping them committed to the program.

Injunctive policies

Injunctive policies require a particular performance target on the part of individual economic agents. Injunctive policies are often referred to as regulations. In contrast to the volitional component of facilitative and inducing policies, here we encounter compulsion.

While compulsion can work quite well in mature and highly articulated nation-states, the history of compulsion in the developing world is problematic. After all, why should new regulations work when so many other aspects of these economies often do not work? It is important to resist seeing these as failed states. These are weak states, and weak states do what they can with the resources at their disposal. As above, these are notional states.

The essential lesson for efforts to bring about changes in environmental behaviors is that such programs will fail if they focus inordinate attention on particular physical attributes of the local environment that happen also to be essential to the livelihood prospects for those who occupy the suddenly favored ecosystems. We use the term *inverse high-grading* to denote a situation in which the desires of outside interests manage to trump the livelihood priorities of humans living in the same vicinity. Of course there will be concern that complementary efforts must be made to improve livelihoods. But the emphasis will often be clear that policy is driven by doing what is necessary—but not much more—for people in order that they will be nice to the parts of nature identified by outsiders as warranting extraordinary protection.

The problem with much biodiversity policy is that it is focused on certain charismatic plants and animals, and it disregards local people who must make a living in the same habitat now considered essential for preserving biodiversity. The two essential decision agents in these systems—those from outside who seek to manipulate local ecosystems, and the local people who must make a living there—face choice sets that are exceedingly fragile concerning long-run success. Notice that the process often starts by the setting of a policy target—a binding constraint—with respect to certain attributes of the local environment, and an associated commitment to prevent deviation from that target. With that constraint in place, local people are then said to be free to go about making a living. Of course this newly imposed institutional regime will often render local people marginalized, and therefore it cannot be a surprise that with the passage of time there will be poaching or a general failure to abide by the agreed-upon ecological targets.

Fortunately, this flawed incentive structure can be improved by a few quite intuitive institutional innovations. For instance, the policy reform process must start by specifying a range of livelihood strategies and plausible implications for local ecological attributes thought to be under threat. This approach could then be rendered more useful by developing a family of plausible development strategies, implied income scenarios, and then working out the implications for biodiversity—or other goals—in the immediate region. That is, policy makers could formulate several development strategies that would evolve as the economic circumstances of the local population evolved. Then, as these livelihood patterns undergo gradual change, it would be possible to connect those livelihood strategies with correlated biodiversity policies that seemed to be consistent with those evolving livelihood trajectories.

Rather than local biodiversity being protected by a right protected by an inalienability rule, the livelihood prospects of local people could be assured under a right protected by a liability rule (Bromley 1991). This second legal regime means that if government programs fail to produce an acceptable income trajectory for local families then the government would be obligated to step up its efforts—that is, to bear financial liability for its failed performance. That obligation would persist until the targeted livelihood results were achieved. Elephant numbers in Southern Africa are now increasingly robust. Meanwhile, it is difficult to suggest that rural livelihoods in the same regions of Southern Africa are at all salutary. Programs to protect desired ecological settings and circumstances will be more successful if they offer livelihood assurances to local people.

What options exist to offer some assurance that local livelihoods are to be plausibly protected? One approach would allow local people to harvest wildlife and cultivate their crops as they see fit. This would not include the right to kill protected animals for objects such as rhinoceros horn or ivory. But killing would be permitted for obtaining bush meat and to reduce the level of serious crop damage. The key to institutional innovation in such settings, whether the resumption of whaling, or the management of wildebeest in Kenya and Tanzania, or the new-found wildlife bounty in southern Sudan, is to incorporate local populations into the new management regime. Local people must be at the core of biodiversity policies rather than being seen as extraneous forces that are somehow inconvenient with respect to some set of desired policies. It is a testament to the great difficulty here that the once-glowing prospects for the CAMPFIRE program in Zimbabwe have not been sustainable (Balint and Mashinya 2006).

Barrett and Arcese (1998) point out the fragile nature of the Integrated Conservation and Development Projects (ICDPs). These programs have failed because they were predicated on a flawed presumption concerning which aspect of the local economy of nature—particular plants and animals or people—ought to be granted rights protected by an inalienability rule (Bromley 1991). But if those who value particular ecological services, and the local people who live in those special places, were accorded certain rights protected by a liability rule, the long-run situation might be improved. This legal structure guides the international regime governing oil spills. That is, rights protected by a liability rule assure victims of environmental assaults—oil spills, poaching—that their losses will be indemnified. The perpetrator of the environmental insult is held liable for actual harms. The rights of the victim are protected by a liability rule for the perpetrator.

Under rights protected by a liability rule, the local people would go about their business fully aware that if unwanted damage occurs to particular parts of the ecosystem the responsible party would be liable for restitution. Similarly, if wildlife cause damage to gardens, crops, or infants, the government (and those outside interests advocating protection of particular ecosystem attributes) would be liable for damage claims. And, if damage runs in the other direction—local people taking too many animals and threatening the long-run trajectory of mutually agreed-upon wildlife numbers—then they (the locals) must be made liable for that damage. Perhaps some of the proceeds from the sale of meat, and perhaps a portion of entrance fees to parks (if a park is nearby), could comprise an escrow account for payments to local people when wildlife numbers are kept within some band of acceptability.

We may think of this as adaptive management with appropriate legal sanctions. Adaptive management entails the core idea that we can never be sure about our policy models and their implications (Walters 1986). In economics this is addressed through an approach recognizing model uncertainty and it evolves through a process of *model averaging* (Brock and Durlauf 2001; Brock, Durlauf, and West 2003). With adaptive management, policy makers must be explicit about the assumptions and predictions so that learning takes place through time. There is a related need to be clear about the nature and extent of uncertainty in the system under study, that uncertainty must be considered along with reference to competing hypotheses, and the policy reform process must give rise to policies that allow quick and low-cost correction. The key here is to avoid policy lock-in (policy path dependence).

As we emphasize throughout, the most coherent stance is to approach policy formulation as an iterative process of searching, dialogue, compromise, and eventual agreement to try something to see how it works. This necessity flows from the ineluctable fact that we do not know what we want until we begin the difficult work of figuring out what it is we seem able to have (Bromley 2006). There can be no plausible answer to the question: "What is the right—or optimal—number of wildebeest on the Serengeti?" But there is an answer to the question: "In a setting of severe uncertainty, in which future states of nature are not only unknown but probably unknowable, what decision algorithm will help us to achieve plausible conservation outcomes?" That decision algorithm would acknowledge complexity, it would recognize that local people must be embedded in the democratic decision protocols, and it would be structured so that learning and feedback are incorporated into the iterative process of working toward what seems possible to achieve.

Rehabilitating dysfunctional irrigation systems

It may seem ironic that irrigation systems are arenas in which economic vulnerability is often magnified by the mutual dependence inherent in such systems. Irrigation water in developing countries is used under a variety of property regimes (Bromley 2000). On surface irrigation systems, government ownership and control of the water usually ends at the point where water enters the main distribution channel for a specific system. From that point forward it is managed, often without much success, by the irrigators themselves. Groundwater is generally owned by the state, but the record of sustainable management of this renewable resource is not encouraging. Because governments have declared authority over an asset that many of them are unable to manage and regulate, depletion of underground stocks is quite common.

In some countries ownership of land bestows title to subsurface water. However, groundwater stocks do not follow parcel demarcation on the surface and so the pumping by one landowner invariably imposes costs on adjoining landowners. Just as with the cost-shifting cement factory in Ghana, each farmer with a tubewell has a tendency to disregard the interests of others who also pump from the same aquifer. However, unlike the cement factory–farmer case, groundwater management is an instance of fully reciprocal externalities—there is no clear villain, or clear victim. Each farmer who pumps underground water is guilty of shifting costs to other farmers who are themselves pumping and shifting costs to others (who also pump).

To see this, imagine that water-pumping technology were of such a scale (and cost) that a large group of farmers needed to pool their funds to acquire such technology. In that case they would have incentives to coordinate their use of the technology (pumps) in order to enhance their collective economic welfare. Surface irrigation systems have this property. Specifically, a surface irrigation system locks a group of farmers together in a regime of mutual (though asymmetric) interdependence. As with river pollution, upstream irrigators on a system are free to disregard the interests of those downstream. The government-provided distribution system acts as the indivisible technology that brings water to the head of a system. Farmers are locked together in a set of reciprocal relations that we find in common property regimes. That is, the group of farmers has the right to exclude others (those not served by the distribution system) from getting water. This is a right sanctioned and supported by the irrigation authority and the national (or state) government. Those who are not situated on the irrigation system (the outsiders) have a duty to abide by that exclusion. However, within the system, individual farmers stand in a position of mutual rights and duties with respect to use rates and maintenance of the system. We see that farmers situated on a surface irrigation system stand united against outsiders, but they are bound together by the reciprocal obligations and expectations of the technological imperative (the distribution system) that brings them the water they all need.

Notice that farmers at or near the head of the system have a clear advantage over those further down the distribution system. These "head-enders" are the first to have water in the main channel flowing past their land, and they also stand insulated from the problems of water leakage and weeds that impede the delivery of water to farmers further down the system. Perhaps most important, those at or near the head of a system have fewer irrigators upstream who might steal water from the main ditch that connects all of them together.

The policy problem in surface irrigation systems is to make sure that the competitive behavior among farmers does not play out in the illicit taking of water out of turn, or in excess of their approved allotment. Equitable water allocation within a system gives each farmer an equal chance to excel at being a farmer, not at figuring out how to take as much water as possible from neighbors. Indeed one of the most undesirable outcomes of dysfunctional surface water systems is that some of the richer farmers defect from the surface system and install their own tubewells and pumps so as to secure reliable water supplies. Notice that this move simply shifts the potential externalities among farmers on the surface system to assured externalities in the underground aquifer.

Consider the issue of equity in water deliveries on a surface irrigation system. The percentage of land to be irrigated can be plotted on the x axis, while the percent of water actually delivered to individual farms during a growing season can be plotted on the vertical axis. Assume that all farmers on a particular irrigation system are equally efficient in their use of water as an agricultural input. This means that there are no efficiency problems in water application among the group of farmers. In other words, each farmer has an equal *efficiency claim* on a unit of water per unit of land under his control. In Figure 6.3 we see two possible situations. The curve E* depicts an allocation of water that approaches complete equity (the heavy line) in water allocation within the system, while E depicts a situation in which 50 percent of the land receives only 20 percent of the available water. At the other extreme, a few farmers—inevitably those at the head of the system—are able to monopolize water receipts such that, in this case, the land they control (the remaining 50 percent) receives 80 percent of the available water.

An important role for policy reform is to modify the institutional arrangements among irrigators in a way that will assure equal water deliveries down through the system. The solution is to place emphasis on the design of an allocation rule—think of it as a constitution—that would create the proper incentives for a system of mutually reinforcing reciprocity.

For settings in which all farmers rely exclusively on groundwater there may be some potential to develop policies that will improve the management of underground water. Notice that if all of the pumping from an aquifer is done by one

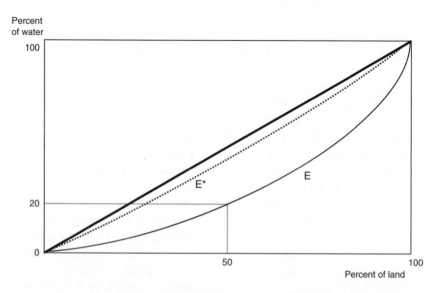

FIGURE 6.3 Toward equity in water deliveries

individual then that individual need only consider his own preferences to decide on the rate at which water will be taken. Here we encounter the popular myth that a single owner of a renewable natural resource has an irresistible incentive to be a good steward of that resource. However, a single owner of a natural resource faces a decision problem that is driven by weighing income now versus income in the future. If the owner has a rate of time preference that is higher than the growth in the present value of future income from the natural resource then the dominant incentive will be to liquidate (take all of) the natural resource and use the revenue for immediate consumption, or invest that revenue in a higher-yield activity (Clark 1973). This problem is called the "iron law of the discount rate" (Page 1977).

However, a distinct management advantage emerges when there are a number of farmers pumping from an aquifer because individuals are situated over varying depths of the aquifer. Those with shallow drafts will be the first to notice excessive withdrawals and can alert others to potential water shortages. Each farmer, while obviously interested in pumping, also has an interest in making sure that he is not disadvantaged by the pumping of others. While individuals are inclined to ignore the costs of their behavior on others, they are not inclined to ignore the costs of others' behavior on them. This is one of the management advantages of a regime of reciprocal externalities; a community of water extractors can actually become a community of water guardians. The policy challenge is to figure out how to instill that response.

Many economists will suggest a pricing scheme for irrigation water. The presumption is that pricing will insure that water is efficiently used in agriculture, and that its use in agriculture vis-à-vis other uses is optimal. That is, water pricing can be thought of as a means to assure that irrigation water is efficiently allocated across all possible uses, as well as across regions, irrigation systems, farmers, soil conditions, and crops. Indeed, most models of optimal pricing regimes tend to see water pricing as a critical factor in assuring that irrigation water, along with other inputs, is optimally utilized on individual farms as well as throughout an irrigation system. When that occurs, all inputs will be efficiently combined to grow the optimal crops in the optimal proportions given the managerial attributes of the system. This approach sees water management as an agricultural problem, and it seeks to make sure that the mix of water use in agriculture and competing demands is efficient. The argument will be advanced that because water is under-priced in agriculture—and it surely is in most settings—getting its price right would induce all-around efficiency in a nation's (or at least a region's) water sector.

But a more practical management idea should not be ruled out. That practical policy reform would seek to insure that water allocation within an irrigation system (or a community of irrigators) is optimal with respect to the efficient and equitable operation of the system as a domain of shared access to a scarce and valuable natural resource. For instance, assume that a known stock of surface water is available for a cropping season, and further assume that this tranche of water is allotted to an irrigation system by a central authority on the basis of one unit of water (w) for each unit of land (L) in each irrigation system. Third, assume that the community of irrigators is bound together by the recognized need to maintain the collective infrastructure represented by the distribution system and the drainage facilities. With each unit (hectare) of land entitled to a certain share of water for the season, the farmer with Li units of land can use all of that water on all of the land under his control, or he can allocate his available water (w) to but a fraction of his total land. If he wants to grow a crop that is highly water-intensive—paddy, sugarcane—then it will likely require that some portion of his land remain dry. The farmer knows how many units of water he will get for the season and it is his choice how that water shall be used. He may also sell that allotment to others on the system, but not outside of the system.

So the irrigation system receives W units of water, where $W = (w \bullet \Sigma Li)$. In essence, individual farmers are shareholders at the beginning of each irrigation system—with the shares to which they are entitled being their proportionate share of W. The management problem becomes a challenge of making sure that the available water (W) is allocated among shareholders in an optimal fashion.

The potential for free-riding on an irrigation system is solved if there is a surcharge applied to each irrigator to reflect the marginal costs imposed on downstream irrigators. The optimal irrigation system is one in which each irrigator along the distribution channel behaves in full knowledge of that marginal cost, and acts so as not to impose external costs on others in the system. That is, perfect compliance with the idea of a unified system is the operational goal of all farmers on the system. We might think of this compliance in terms of each farmer's contribution to the public good that is the efficient operation of the system. If that is attained then all water-use externalities will disappear.

Notice that we have here an institutional challenge that is related to the optimal provision of a public good. The public good in this system has several components. First, the public good is represented by the allocation of water down through the system that solves the problem of equality of marginal costs for each farmer in obtaining water. Second, the public good is a maintenance program for the entire system that involves all farmers in routine upkeep such that the level of water yield at each water intake on the system is optimal. Finally, the public good is a schedule of groundwater pumping by individual irrigators that is both consistent with the sustainable yield of the underlying aquifer, and that makes each irrigator conscious of the marginal costs of the choice between using groundwater and using surface water.

The public good within an irrigation system is therefore the attainment of optimal behaviors across four interrelated margins (realms): (1) efficiency in water allocation along a channel; (2) efficiency in system maintenance; (3) efficiency in groundwater extraction; and (4) efficiency in the conjunctive use of surface water and groundwater. The more of the public good that is provided, the better the system will perform in terms of water yield at each water intake, in terms of reduced externalities along the distribution channel, in terms of system maintenance, and in terms of the conjunctive use of groundwater and surface water. This would represent the optimal provision of the public good.

The institutional innovation could be in the form of a financial assessment at the start of each season, plus the quantity of donated time for system maintenance over some defined period of time. This could be a water charge levied on each irrigator.

The proper fee would reflect the preferences of all farmers on the system for all-around efficiency in terms of net water yield at each farmer's water intake, system maintenance, conjunctive use of groundwater and surface water, as well as assurance that each farmer's water receipts exactly match his proportionate share (his entitlement) (Baland and Platteau 1996). If the irrigation system is characterized by anarchy then the public good is underprovided and eventually the system will cease to function. Under a regime of full positive reciprocity, every farmer does exactly as all others do—this can range from anarchy to full (optimal) individual provision of the public good.

The management problem then concerns how to induce each farmer to contribute exactly the correct amount. That amount is the monetary value (or labor equivalent) of each farmer's willingness to pay to have the system function optimally. It is also the amount that each farmer will want every other farmer to contribute to the provision of the public good. That is, each farmer knows that unless all contribute this amount, the system will not perform as each farmer wants it to perform—some farmers will receive less water than their entitlement, some will shirk on their maintenance obligation and cause excessive water loss for others, some will extract too much from the groundwater aquifer, or some will not make the efficient choice between using surface water and groundwater (Sugden 1984). To Sugden the principle of reciprocity requires that each individual contribute to the public good exactly that amount which each would most prefer every member of the group to contribute. Sugden argues that since self-interest within the limits of reciprocity is assumed here, each irrigator has an obligation to himself to contribute at least as much as self-interest requires.

In operational terms we might think of this optimal contribution to the public good as *earnest money* on the part of each farmer; it must be paid before an irrigation season starts. This payment would not go to the irrigation administration for the delivery of water to the system. Rather, this payment is the annual fee that is required of each farmer in order to receive water during the coming season. That is, the contribution is required before the irrigation season starts. The charge must be understood to encompass maintenance of the system as well as for the water made available to the farmer by the community of irrigators, not by the national water authority. Recall that the community of irrigators—a water users' association—cannot avoid anarchy unless it assesses such charges before the growing season gets underway. If liquidity before the crop season is a problem for some poorer farmers, the system can have some built in slack that will cover necessary costs for a few farmers during the irrigation season.

The resource curse

Many developing countries rely almost exclusively on the export of natural resources for the production of necessary revenues for the government. Indeed, one knowledgable observer has written:

> There is a long history of the idea that there is some strong, consistent connection between the ways in which governments are financed and the ways

in which they govern…There is also a more theoretical tradition of academic work that links long-term changes in society and governance to changes in the ways in which states obtain the resources they need to govern. Its leading exponents also see close affinities between the dependence of governments on general taxation, modern capitalism, and liberal democracy.

(Moore 2007: 80)

Moore elaborates the above idea by suggesting: "Dependence on general taxation provides incentives for state elites and taxpayers to resolve their differences through bargaining" (Moore 2007: 84). On the contrary, when governments in developing countries do not rely on general taxation, but instead derive their necessary revenues from: (1) export or import taxes; (2) surpluses arising from monopoly (state) control of agricultural surpluses; (3) surpluses arising from trade in consumer goods; (4) surpluses from state property; or (5) from the export of natural resources such as oil, timber, fish, or minerals, those governments have little need to engage the broader citizenry in the business of governance. General taxes on income and wealth—the tax bargain—must be understood as an essential aspect of improved governance and hence of development.

The core idea behind the tax bargain is that all governments and their citizens necessarily engage in continual bargaining over the control of financial resources. Individuals earn incomes from those economic activities that are sanctioned by the state. The state, in its commitments to such collective-consumption goods as roads, rail lines, general communications networks, the judicial system, police, and what is now called the rule of law, requires financial resources to deliver those goods and services. Citizens need the services of government and the government needs to make sure that citizens are satisfied with the delivery of goods and services so that the required resources continue to be forthcoming. Legislatures are the locus of this bargaining. Some interests wish for less government and lower taxes while others see a more expansive role for government which implies higher taxes. It is necessary to understand that countries are domains of redistribution, and much of that redistributive debate centers on these contested issues.

In most states, with taxation falling on individuals in the form of annual assessments against income and/or wealth, there is a mutuality of interests. Improving economic conditions across the political landscape bring benefits to individuals and households, and those improving conditions then yield greater revenue to the government. The underlying incentives, therefore, induce both parties to the tax bargain—politicians and citizens—to support policies that will encourage growth. Of course their common interests diverge over the taxes that will be levied against individual (household) gains from that growth. However, the dominant incentive lies in the direction of increasing the private income position of the individual or household, and only then arguing about what share of that new increment will be taxed away. Notice that when taxes are not levied as a share of personal income and wealth the mutuality of interests is missing. In the absence of this key nexus, political elites lack a commitment to economic prosperity among the general population and will focus their attention instead on other means by which they alone might benefit financially—even though the nation as a whole is not doing well. It is here that the concern for corruption emerges.

A second incentive property of the tax bargain is that when the provision of goods and services is supported from general tax revenues—as opposed to import or export taxes—there is constant pressure on the government to improve the efficacy with which it delivers those goods and services. If the citizens are paying taxes directly tied to the expected delivery of a bundle of goods and services they are likely to be more demanding of government to make sure that it is acting in accord with those expectations.

Third, this aspect also serves to draw citizens more directly into the broader political arena to make them more involved across a wide range of issues. We see that the tax bargain is really part of the broader *citizenship bargain*. In other words, making citizens pay brings them more directly into the broader arena of governance and political attentiveness. It is to be expected that the degree of government accountability will increase.

However, the resource curse arises in situations in which the political elite are often quite satisfied to be insulated from the demands of the citizenry. If their economic interests can be met by import and export taxes they do not need to devote much attention to the concerns of those thinly scattered across the rural hinterland. The tax bargain works to render this political and economic estrangement less acceptable. And when political and economic estrangement is reduced, economic coherence inevitably increases.

The tax bargain is a good example of institutional change that would bring about less reliance on natural resource extraction, and it would therefore connect the citizenry more closely with the important matter of governance. In that sense, the tax bargain holds important implications for both vulnerable people and for vulnerable states.

In states with weak taxing powers, and therefore weak obligations to individual citizens, it is clear that vulnerability is a serious problem. In such settings, citizens are largely irrelevant to the central government. But an equal vulnerability is apparent at the level of the nation-state. Undue reliance on a narrow idiosyncratic source of resource rents exposes the state to swings in global prices and global demands for the single dominant export—oil, timber, or minerals. Dependence on resource extraction is never a good economic strategy, and it is a worse political strategy.

While broadening the tax base through the tax bargain will not be easy to implement, a gradual shift away from near-total reliance on natural resource extraction would pay a double dividend. First it would blunt the pressure on governments to rely on resource extraction for necessary funding of government services, and it would therefore serve to dampen the incentives to destroy biodiversity and other natural assets. Second, by gradually bringing individuals into the citizenship bargain, governments would become more accountable for the level and quality of services delivered to the citizenry.

While these institutional changes would be of great help, there is a more vexing aspect of the resource curse and that is the problem of dependency. That dependency can take several forms. As above, it can be a dependency on the receipts from resource extraction that drives a wedge between a government and its citizens. Another dependency is one that concerns linkages to a foreign government that may come to hold undue political influence in the future. We see this in current discussions about the growing presence of China in sub-Saharan Africa. Put in historical context, this is an ironic concern. During the height of the Cold War the U.S. and the Soviet Union both perfected the craft of clientelism—keeping particular poor countries financially dependent in exchange for their claimed political alliances. Now that China is becoming more prominent in African affairs, it seems disingenuous for traditional regional players to complain.

The more serious problem with the resource curse is that the generous earnings from exports tend to discourage other investment in the economy. This dampening of investment happens because the rates of return on other commercial investments look so meager compared with returns from the export sector that credit markets discourage these alternative activities. So the economy remains narrowly focused on just one or two profitable export opportunities and fails to expand into other necessary economic activities. Associated with this tendency is the emergence of a rentier class of local citizens who live on resource royalties and the correlated need for immigrant labor to attend to the normal jobs required in an economy—drivers, engineers, teachers, mechanics, skilled craftsmen, and the like. In many situations, the natural resource sector is an enclave having minimal interaction with the rest of the economy (Collier 2007; Sachs and Warner 2001).

Improving markets across space

A common problem in developing countries is that markets fail to work well across space. And when markets do not work across space, individual and household vulnerabilities are exacerbated. Often, rural households will, of necessity, withdraw into autarky. Without feasible access to a range of market possibilities, households are unable to shield or diversify their exposure to a variety of risks—fluctuating prices, fluctuating yields, and fluctuating non-farm employment prospects.

We can analyze these problems in terms of high transaction costs. Recall that transaction costs entail information costs, contracting costs, and enforcement costs. In Figure 6.4 we depict a classic von Thünen land-rent model with three distinct regions: (1) urban; (2) peri-urban, and (3) rural.

First, consider the rent gradient R. This curve depicts the net economic value of land uses as one moves out from the central business district of a large city in the developing world. With high transaction costs the income potential diminishes rapidly as one leaves the urban core. The diminishment in the economic value of land is reflective of transportation costs to move goods to and from remote rural places. But more is at work here. Specifically, if there is poor market news out in rural areas, if legal protections are minimal, if the physical infrastructure (roads, bridges) is

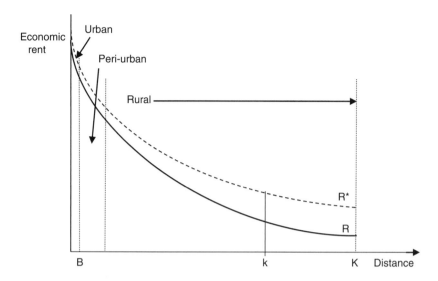

FIGURE 6.4 Actual and the counterfactual rent gradients

degraded, if theft in transit is a problem, and if spoilage degrades fresh products as they move to urban markets—many of the same problems faced by Kweku Owiredu—the net income available from parcels of agricultural land will be depressed. With low income potential, it cannot be a surprise that economic activity diminishes as one moves out and away from the major center. Investment in such places is unrewarding. We would say that the rural economy is operating in a *state of nature* where high transaction costs stifle most entrepreneurial activity (Bromley 2008a; Kronman 1985; Bromley and Chavas 1989).

Leaving aside for now the poor quality of physical infrastructure, notice that a program to reduce transaction costs could work to improve the legal regime radiating out from urban markets. If the institutional reforms are successful we can depict a second rent gradient R*. This enhanced rent gradient reflects an improved institutional setting for agricultural markets in which transportation systems are safe and reliable, communication options are ubiquitous and affordable, legal services are present and trustworthy, and credit and product markets are prevalent and function with considerable efficiency. In other words, policy reform brings good governance to the rural hinterland. And that enhanced governance makes investment a rewarding activity. Soon, economic activity would begin to grow and spread.

Let us consider the following question: "What would it be worth, in economic terms, for producers in remote rural areas to enjoy approximately the same level of coherent governance as that enjoyed in the distant urban center?" We can demonstrate the answer to this important question by comparing the two rent gradients in Figure 6.4.

The rent gradient R* in Figure 6.4 depicts the *rent possibilities frontier* under a feasible regime of economic coherence across space. While R* is simply one of a family of possible gradients, we may consider it an idealized gradient depicting the net income possibilities of rural producers under the assumption of improved institutional arrangements concerning the movement, contracting over, and disposition of goods produced in the rural economy. The difference between the existing rent gradient (R) and the rent possibilities frontier (R*) shows the plausible net economic gains from coherent governance as measured against the status quo institutional setup. This magnitude can be considered as the economic benefits of improved coherence.

Let φ_k depict the extent to which the current net income (rent) potential of a unit of land is reduced by the absence of coherent governance at distance k from the capital city, where:

$$0 \leq \varphi_k < 1 \tag{6.1}$$

When $\varphi_k \approx 0$ the income potential of a unit of land approaches that possible under an idealized governance regime offering a bundle of goods and services designed to encourage and support investment and entrepreneurial activity. On the other hand, if the current governance situation in the hinterland is deleterious—if there is economic incoherence—then $\varphi_k \approx 1$ and the current rent gradient R is pertinent. We can write the net rent available from a hectare of land at point k as:

$$R = Q\left[(p_t - \varphi_k) - TC\right] - Qck \tag{6.2}$$

where Q is the average yield of a hectare of land at k, p_t is the sale price of that unit of produce in the urban center, φ_k is an index of the depreciation caused by the absence of good governance at point k, TC is the average total and variable cost of producing a unit of Q at point k, c is the transport costs per unit of Q per unit of distance from the urban center, and k is distance from the urban center. Notice that when $\varphi_k = 0$ equation (6.2) reduces to the counterfactual rent possibilities gradient (R* in Figure 6.4), but that when φ_k takes on values greater than zero then the inferior gradient R becomes a plausible depiction of the situation in many rural markets.

We see that φ_k can be thought of as a measure of the private opportunity cost to the individual agricultural producer situated at point k from having to operate under an institutional regime displaying incoherence. This implies, therefore, that φ_k is an index of the private willingness to pay of an individual firm located at k to be able to undertake economic activity in a regime of economic coherence. If we imagine a large number of individuals (N) seeking to make a living situated k units from the capital city, then equation (6.3)

$$\sum_{i=1}^{N} \varphi_{i,k} \tag{6.3}$$

is an indexed transformation of the aggregate willingness to pay on the part of all individuals located at distance k from the central city to engage in economic activity parameterized by a coherent institutional regime. If we want to think of this willingness to pay encompassing all individuals beyond the boundary (B) of the urban center, and extending to the national frontier (K) then equation (6.4) is of interest.

$$\sum_{i=1}^{N}\sum_{k=B}^{K}\varphi_{i,k} \tag{6.4}$$

This illustration demonstrates that there are very real private and social costs to institutional incoherence that exists in rural agricultural markets (Bromley and Foltz 2011). It also demonstrates the role of careful diagnostics as a necessary precursor to the design of development assistance efforts concerned with vulnerable people and vulnerable states.

Implications

The vulnerability of individuals and households is a reflection of the extent to which a national economy can be said to cohere. And the nature and specific attributes of a particular nation's economy are simply manifestations of its institutional architecture. These institutional arrangements define realms of individual and group action. In economic terminology, the institutional arrangements define the choice sets available to individuals. When social and economic outcomes are judged to be undesirable it is necessary that the choice sets from which individuals may select their preferred economizing actions must be modified in some manner. In that sense, problematic outcomes have their probable causes in the individual behaviors enabled (authorized) by the decision space available to individual decision makers. Economic policy reforms therefore entail a gradual redefinition of the decision space available to individuals. In practical terms: "You must no longer pollute and others will no longer be forced to bear your shifted costs. You are now constrained, and they are now liberated." We refer to such institutional changes as policy reform. That is, policy reform is concerned with alterations in the institutional architecture of a nation-state.

We have presented five situations of flawed social and economic outcomes, and we have traced those unwanted outcomes to the underlying institutional arrangements that provide the basis for the incentives operating on individuals in the economy. Each illustration captures a different form of economic incoherence. The essential lesson here is that individuals behave for a reason—or for a combination of reasons—and therefore the most effective way to mitigate unwanted social and economic outcomes is to alter the incentive structure that is instrumental in producing those outcomes. Those who work on policy reform must always pay careful attention to the causal structure underlying individual and group behavior, and efforts to change that behavior.

Our first illustration concerned the classic pollution problem. In this situation of negative externalities, it is easy for individual firms to ignore the off-site costs imposed on others by activities of the polluting firms. In Figures 6.1 and 6.2 these flawed institutions—in the absence of a law against the emission of pollutants—result in excessive total output of the polluting industry and the correlated burden of costs falling on others. Mr. Owiredu's tomatoes were ruined before he could get them to market. Policy reform in this setting might entail the prohibition of pollutants, the imposition of a fee on every unit of pollutant dumped, or the facilitation of bargaining and negotiations among all participants in this unwelcome setting. The purpose of policy reform here is to rectify the presence and incidence of external costs by forcing polluters to internalize these unwanted social costs. Doing so brings economic coherence.

The second illustration concerned economic schemes to create incentives for local people to become more directly engaged in the sustainable management of environmental resources. In some instances this involvement might concern efforts to mitigate specific harmful practices. In other instances this involvement might concern new behaviors that seem to hold promise for improving local environmental practices and outcomes. Policy reform will figure prominently in each of these possible initiatives. Perhaps payments will be offered to local people to deflect their current practices onto more benign pathways. Perhaps other incentives can be formulated that will draw them into activities that hold promising outcomes. The policy challenge in such programs is to makes sure that funds are targeted and that those funds yield program objectives at the lowest possible cost. There is a sustainability challenge as well—changing economic and ecological circumstances means that all contracts must be constantly reassessed and modified as conditions warrant.

The irrigation problem is a classic "free-rider" dilemma. How can policy reform improve the coordination failures that plague all such systems? Care is required to assess the power differential along the distribution channels, and to overcome the locational advantages that exist on such systems. Often it will help to create an institutional structure that negates physical advantage on a system so that each irrigator on a system is exposed to the potential threat of shirking and free-riding by others. If this situation can figure prominently in the process of institutional innovation, it will be possible to make progress in rectifying the current problems of dysfunction and inequity. In many respects, the incentives and governance procedures within surface irrigation systems are a microcosm of institutional and governance problems in the larger economy. It will be impossible to rectify these incoherencies in individual irrigation systems without, at the same time, introducing parallel policy reforms in the broader society. Each venue of reform will inform and support reforms in the other.

The fourth illustration concerned the resource curse. Here the central problem is that governments are unable to create and benefit from a broad and inclusive tax base to underwrite the necessary funding of essential government services. As a result, governments become dependent on one or two dominant export sectors for the bulk of their operational revenue. The corrosive effects on good governance, and the potential for corruption, are thereby exacerbated. Unfortunately, the standard mantra of eliminating corruption is focused on the symptoms of this problem rather than on the root of the problem. Policy reform in this instance concerns a search for ways to broaden the tax base so that all citizens become engaged in the necessary activity of paying for government services, and placing demands on government when those services do not measure up to what the citizenry expects in returns for its taxation. Bringing scattered individuals into the citizenship bargain is a promising way to meliorate the many problems of vulnerable people and vulnerable states.

The final illustration concerned a somewhat related problem—that of institutional attenuation across space that defeats private economic prospects for vulnerable people. In essence, many countries are unable to extend the reach of institutional coherence across vast distances, and this inability then stifles economic activity across space. Rural economic productivity suffers twice—the resource base may be inadequate, and the problems of legal (institutional) dysfunction as one moves away from the central city suppress net income prospects across a range of economic pursuits. With indifferent rewards for investment and entrepreneurial initiative, individual families retreat into autarky. Their economic situation settles into bare subsistence, there is no latitude for initiative, and they remain highly vulnerable. Such circumstances often breed resignation among the elderly, and frustration among the young. The prevalence of civil strife across Africa and the Middle East is no mystery. It is not poverty that threatens notional states. Rather, it is the absence of hope among the young. The profound revolutionary changes in early 2011 across North Africa demonstrate the predicted result of vulnerable people and vulnerable states.

There are many examples we could draw upon to illuminate the connection between particular institutional arrangements, the perverse incentives they present to atomistic decision makers, and the unwanted social and economic outcomes that result from the maximizing decisions of millions of individuals in an economy. Gaining an understanding of the diagnostic imperative allows us now to take the next step—policy reform in the service of addressing vulnerable people and vulnerable states.

7

FROM DIAGNOSIS TO POLICY REFORM

We could know *a priori* that a thought was true only if its truth was to be recognized from the thought itself (without an object of comparison).
(Ludwig Wittgenstein, Tractatus Logico-Philosophicus, 3.05)

Policy diagnostics

As emphasized in the previous chapter, the purpose of policy diagnostics is to gain an understanding of something we want to know, but do not, from what we think we know, but are not quite sure. For those who work in the area of development assistance, the explicit purpose of policy diagnostics is to determine why particular individuals in a given sector—agriculture, transportation, food processing and marketing—are unable to realize and sustain enhanced household incomes. Economic incoherencies defeat a family's aspirations for an improved future. Policy diagnostics starts from the presumption that unpromising livelihoods are not the fault of the individuals who find themselves economically marginalized. Rather, policy diagnostics presumes that members of particular households are devoted to improving their economic circumstances but encounter persistent constraints in that quest. This assumption is required for the simple reason that changes in policy cannot possibly help those for whom current policies are not a binding constraint. Policy diagnostics, therefore, is focused on identifying the constraints that prevent motivated and committed individuals from improving their incomes and thus enhancing their life prospects.

For Kweku Owiredu, and millions of individuals in similar circumstances, economic survival is a constant struggle—not because his management skills are defective. Kweku is marginalized because nothing in his economic existence seems to work well. Some problems are visited upon him—pollution from the cement factory, impossible roads during the wet season, delays and bribery when he seeks to move his vegetables to market, and pest infestations. For some other constraints, they are problematic not because they are intrusive but because they are missing when needed. For these matters, he merely needs a little help from others—access to an agricultural extension agent, a more reliable supply of electricity, a more effective surface irrigation system, plausible supplies of groundwater, reliable fertilizer supplies, and access to production credit. Each of these problems (shown in Figure 7.1) seriously constrains his farming operation and they therefore defeat, in their own way, his chances to succeed.

In the previous chapter we introduced a concept that we now shall call *layered diagnostics*. That is, the process of policy reform must attend to layers of impediments that defeat economic coherence—this is in reference to *A'*, *A''*, and *A'''* from Chapter 6.

In Figure 7.1 these impediments are "first-order" incoherencies for Kweku. We call them "first-order" problems because they are the immediate and obvious impacts experienced by the farm household.

The diagnostic approach is valuable because it reveals these first-order problems, of such importance to Kweku, as merely the symptoms of a variety of analytically prior incoherencies. From this we see that diagnosis necessarily starts with the incidence and extent of the problems facing Kweku and similarly situated individuals, and then continues onward until the "actionable cause" has been identified. This next stage is called "second-order" economic incoherence because it is here that we find the origin of the symptoms that plague Kweku. This stage also highlights the lack of agency facing Kweku. That is, he is unable to have any effects on the origins of the economic incoherence in which he is mired. This second-order problem is depicted in Figure 7.2.

Notice that the policy-relevant incoherencies are found here. These are the reasons why farmers such as Kweku have such difficulties increasing household incomes. Notice that once these explanations have been identified, the task of remediation—policy reform—can get underway.

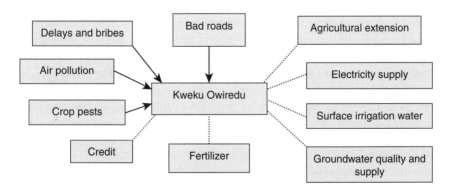

FIGURE 7.1 First-order economic incoherence: dysfunctional exposure

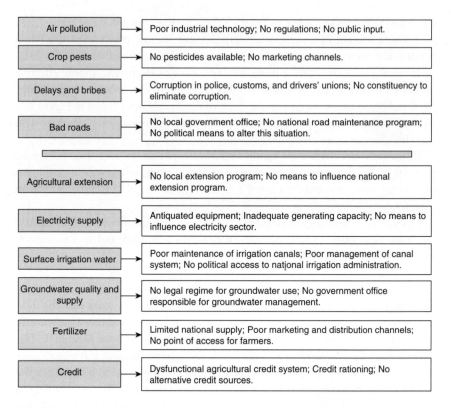

FIGURE 7.2 Second-order economic incoherence: missing agency

The policy-reform process

The problem-solving processes necessarily start with a problematic situation—what Charles Sanders Peirce calls "surprise" and the "irritation of doubt." In the present context, this newly realized problem is simply a specific undesirable social or economic outcome arising from the aggregate of millions of atomistic (individual) choices. It is important to keep in mind that these individual actions occur within a decision space—an opportunity set—that is defined by existing institutional arrangements. Economic theory has taught us to assume that human action is motivated by incentives at the margin—prices and marginal costs. However, the vast majority of human action is habituated—people going about their daily lives as they have been doing for a very long time. Of course prices and costs are often decisive. But much (most?) human action is habituated and based upon a rather more intuitive sense of "maximization." Individuals are rational by being reasonable (Bromley 2006).

In this view, humans select their best actions from within an opportunity set that is omnipresent in their lives, and which is parameterized by prevailing institutional arrangements—norms, conventions, legal rules and property entitlements.

Therefore when the aggregate outcomes of millions of atomistic choices add up to unwelcome results, the inevitable implication is that the decision space of individuals—their choice sets—are revealed to be in need of modification. Policy reform is the process of altering those choice sets through institutional change.

Our approach starts with the existence of certain outcomes—serious deforestation, high unemployment, air pollution, nascent epidemics, declining agricultural yields, widespread hunger, accelerated soil erosion, unsafe drinking water—that are soon realized to be the unwelcome outcomes (symptoms) of a particular constellation of institutional arrangements pertinent to those behaviors. Because institutions are instrumental to choice, these unwanted behaviors (and their consequent outcomes) represent the reason for, the justification of, institutional change (policy reform) that will, if correctly done, rectify these unwanted circumstances. Recognition of particular social or economic problems is thus the essential motivation for policy reform. These undesirable outcomes can be identified as potentially serious by national leaders, local organizations, international donors or NGOs, or individuals such as Kweku Owiredu and his neighbors. As above, rectifying the problem requires institutional change that will create new incentives (and fields of action) that will then inform how organizations and individuals may/may not, can/cannot, and must/must not conduct their independent activities. These new rules (institutions) will also assign new roles and responsibilities for their implementation, monitoring, and enforcement.

Moreover, the new institutional arrangements may also stipulate access to financing and sources of financing (e.g. taxes, fees, and fines). As certain institutions undergo change it may also be the case that new organizations are called for, or that existing organizations will need to be re-structured (or strengthened) in order to implement the new rules. Ultimately, a new set of outcomes will be observed as the plausible result of changes in particular institutions and organizations.

POLICY STATES CONSIST OF

- Current constellation of institutions (rules and laws) and governmental organizational attributes that define individual and collective action
- Current political, economic, social, and cultural contexts
- Outcome of the policy action taken during the associated stage of the policy process

---

The policy reform-process consists of a series of distinct **stages** designed to address a problem through the modification of institutions—new policies—that will redefine and reconstitute particular organizations and their roles, that will engage and enhance the capacities of those organizations, and that will guide individuals in their roles as managers, educators, evaluators, and implementers. Each **stage** is characterized by a distinct set of activities—**policy actions**—that are designed to advance the policy-reform process. At the conclusion of a suite of policy actions we encounter a **policy state**. The policy state summarizes the intermediate results, products and outcomes of the policy actions, as well as clarifying current information and changes in the political, economic, and social contexts that may have changed during the stage of the process. Policy actions are the drivers of the policy-reform process—advancing the process from the policy state at the beginning of the stage to the policy state at the end of the stage. Stages of the policy-reform process are comprised of *actions* and *states* in recognition of the fact that once a policy state is reached, the process can "rest" at that state until additional actions are undertaken. Thus, for each stage, the starting point for policy action is the policy state from the previous stage.

In the context of the policy-reform process, it is useful to regard a specific **problem** (a problematic situation) as the initial **policy state**. That is, all social and economic outcomes are the result of some existing constellation of institutional arrangements. And such constellations of institutions—being the product of an earlier (sometimes much earlier) process of institutional change—are simply policy states in the general sense of that idea. We have a set of outcomes informed by—predicated upon—an existing set of institutional arrangements.

Once a problematic situation has been recognized, and when it has been determined that the problem must be rectified, we enter the first stage of the policy-reform process—**problem diagnosis**. The policy action here is that of **diagnosing**. **Diagnosing** includes a set of activities concerned with collecting and assessing information about the problem (or problems), why the problem exists, identifying potential barriers to new policies, determining which of the identified problems are of highest priority (and policy relevant), and developing a suite of potential policy reforms that might address the high-priority problems. When this stage is complete, the result is the policy state we call **assessment**. This state includes an elaboration of the problem diagnosis, and recommendations for policy reforms. In addition, there is a general stocktaking of the current policy context, as well as an assessment of any institutional changes that might have occurred while the diagnostic activity was under way. This is important since one or more of these intervening changes may well influence the subsequent selection of policies.

The second stage of the policy reform process is termed **policy design**. Here we encounter the policy action of **designing**. At this point in the process, candidate policies are assessed, reviewed, revised, and ultimately selected. The resulting policy state is **new policies** consisting of a complex set of necessary institutional and organizational modifications and adjustments.

The third stage—**implementation**—is often the most difficult aspect of the policy-reform process. The policy action here is **implementing**. Activities here may include the adoption of legal strictures (both parliamentary and administrative), developing an implementation strategy, modifying certain organizations, strengthening particular organizational capacities, mobilizing the necessary financial resources, and establishing a monitoring plan. The successful completion of this action phase results in **policy adoption**. It is here that the new policy reforms will be incorporated into the legal framework (the working rules) of the nation-state. Examples include new laws (or administrative rulings) concerning: (1) discharging pollutants; (2) fertilizer subsidies; (3) deforestation; (4) working conditions in factories; (5) safety standards for trucks; (6) safety inspections in abattoirs; or (7) the chemical content of drinking water.

The formal legislative and administrative adoption of new policies (new institutions) is, however, no assurance that individual behaviors will thereby automatically and instantly change. Recall that new policy is a combination of three things: (1) new desired outcomes in the future; (2) institutional change that will plausibly bring about those outcomes; and (3) enforcement to give those new institutional changes empirical substance. Therefore, policy adoption leads into the fourth stage we call **policy adaptation**. Here, implementing agencies must insure that the formal adoption of new working rules (institutions) and organizational modifications actually occur. The set of policy actions for this stage is termed **adapting**.

We call this stage **policy adaptation** to call attention to fact that here, more than elsewhere in the process, policy-reform must become concerned with changing the way in which individuals go about their daily life. New policies mean that some firms and households will have their domains of choice—their fields of action—modified, and these changes will require adjustment and adaptation. The idea of adaptation also means that individuals who work in various government ministries will likely have their standard routines altered in particular ways. There may be organizational changes requiring that particular employees will be moved around. Laws may require different specialized monitoring. The new institutions and organizational arrangements should, if the process has been well crafted, bring about changes in behaviors and it is expected that these changes will result in new **policy outcomes**.

The final stage is called **evaluation** and the action associated with this stage is that of **evaluating**. In one sense this final stage can be understood as the logical analogue of "problem identification." That is, when the policy reform process appears to have been completed, it is always necessary to assess the extent to which the original problem has actually been solved. We must not assume that this judgment can be rendered immediately. Indeed, problems and vulnerabilities take a long time to emerge and their solution will likewise take a long time to become operational. The assessment of all completed reforms is, in one sense, never finished.

Table 7.1 summarizes the sequence of policy stages, actions, and states that characterize the policy-reform process.

As above, policy reform does not end when the process begins to yield altered policy outcomes. The setting for policy is dynamic—as policy outcomes are observed, decision makers and interested parties will be induced to consider whether or not the policies are still appropriate, and whether or not they are generating the desired, as opposed to undesired, outcomes. In this sense, all participants are necessarily engaged in a process of learning as the policy process moves from stage to stage—adding knowledge and experience gained from the previous stage, and updating contexts and expectations. It is important to understand that desired

TABLE 7.1 Policy stages, actions, and states

Policy stage	Policy action	Policy state
Problem diagnosis	Diagnosing	Assessment
Policy design	Designing	New policies
Implementation	Implementing	Policy adoption
Adaptation	Adapting	Policy outcomes
Evaluation	Evaluating	Judgment

outcomes in the future cannot be known at the time that decisions are undertaken to set a country on a path toward new more desired outcomes. A lengthy reform process, combined with rapidly changing economic and political settings, can result in a set of outcomes that are no longer desired. In practical terms, "the world moves as we are trying to go there." The appropriate analogy is that of aiming a spacecraft at a distant planet—engineers must aim for the exact spot where the planet is expected to be in five or six years.

Embedded in the policy-reform process—and serving to motivate the continuous search for a constellation of new policies, incentives, and sanctions—is the process of *mutual learning*. Discussions of possible actions focused on the future are necessarily exercises in creating plausible empirical claims about that future, and about how best to get there. Since we have not yet lived in the future, each participant in the discourse about the future will bring different ideas about what that future will and ought to entail. And those same individuals will bring distinct ideas about how to alter current institutions and associated patterns of interaction in order that the desired future might actually materialize. The economist G.L.S. Shackle referred to this as a process of "contestation among contending created imaginings" (Shackle 1961). It might also be referred to as prospective volition—considering the future, and figuring out how individuals or groups wish for that future to unfold (Bromley 2006).

The most important aspect of this process in the context of policy reform is to allow all participants to learn as they work their way toward a solution to the problematic situation. Despite how the choice problem is modelled in economics, in reality people work out what they think they want as they engage in the process of working out—often with others in a group setting—what they believe they might be able to have (to get). One does not really know what one wants until they are on the way to figuring out what can be accomplished by specific actions (Bromley 2006, 2008c). Policy reform is, in essence, a collaborative learning exercise—it is the pragmatic consideration of the options people face.

Notice that learning requires constant evaluation of the suitability of outcomes. Evaluation covers a broad range of formal and informal assessments designed to review the performance of the new institutions and organizational changes in terms of how well the outcome accords with *ex ante* expectations. However, notice that evaluation must consider not only how the new policies have performed in terms of criteria used to select the suite of policies during the design stage. Specifically, evaluation must also take into account changes over time in expectations, in the specific political, economic, social, and cultural contexts related to the new polices, and changes in other institutions that directly or indirectly influence the performance of the new policies.

Table 7.2 provides a summary of all the policy actions for the five stages of the policy reform process.

Recall that policy reform starts with a problem—what we earlier called the initial **policy state**. The existence and recognition of a problem inevitably entails an activity called "evaluation." That is, a problem, by definition, is the result of an *evaluative process*.

One can think of policy reform as *adaptive management*. Adaptive management involves adjustments that represent feedback or backward linkages in the policy-reform process. Typically, adaptive responses involve fine-tuning of the policy or its implementation with an emphasis on improving performance of the new policy. For major policies, the prospect of conducting a new problem diagnosis requires a significant commitment of financial resources and time. Thus, one of the challenges of evaluation is to determine if performance of the new policy can be improved through appropriate adaptive responses.

TABLE 7.2 Policy actions

How do you do it?	*Steps*
Diagnosing	Identify problems and assess them in terms of current policies Identify policy options Assess potential barriers and constraints to policies
Designing	Establish the process, criteria, venues, and participants for the vetting and selection of policy choices Assess policy choices; formulate pros and cons, analyze costs and benefits, and elaborate cultural preferences Select new policies
Implementing	Develop implementation strategy that assigns and formalizes organization roles and plans for staff and financial resources for implementing organizations Legalize new policies—codify policies in legislative acts and decrees Prepare administrative rules and procedures
Adapting	Adapt organization capacity to implement new policies Communicate new policies and educate stakeholders on policy provisions Adapt behaviors and adopt or innovate appropriate technologies and practices
Evaluating	Undertake monitoring and assessment activities in light of reform objectives Incorporate new objectives if pertinent, and assess results Reach consensus regarding success or the need for refinement

TABLE 7.3 Best practices for managing the policy-reform process

	Best practices
Build competence (Learning)	1. Identify key interested parties and stakeholders. 2. Engage them in the policy reform process. 3. Promote local ownership of problem diagnosis and of possible reforms. 4. Engage other donors to bolster credibility and policy coherence.
Foster communications (Sharing)	5. Create a climate of open communication. 6. Develop a shared understanding of the policy problem. 7. Assess progress to enhance learning and adaptation. 8. Communicate successes and setbacks with all participants.
Create confidence (Believing)	9. Build trust among all participants. 10. Develop good analytical skills. 11. Use best practices. 12. Draw on early successes to bolster confidence and momentum.

Those engaged in development assistance face the difficult task of managing a process of policy reform that is often challenged by those who enjoy particular advantages in the current situation. Change is never easy, and there will be individuals who find that necessary institutional change is a serious threat to their standard habits of action. It is often the case that reducing vulnerability for particular segments of a population will threaten economic or political advantage for others. Table 7.3 is a brief listing of best practices for managing the policy-reform process, and working with that process.

The point of these 12 suggestions is to focus development assistance on the practical yet necessary aspects of accomplishing policy reform. Tables 7.1 and 7.2 highlight what is to be done in the process of policy reform. Table 7.3 highlights the most important aspects of managing how it is to be done.

Managing the policy-reform process

There are three important aspects to managing the policy-reform process: (1) build competence, which concerns helping host-country counterparts to become better at guiding policy reforms in the future; (2) foster communications, which concerns mutual learning on the part of donors and host-country counterparts; and (3) create confidence, which concerns helping host-country counterparts believe in the importance of policy reform—and their guiding role in it.

Build competence

Identify key interested parties and stakeholders

Perhaps the most important aspect of policy reform is to locate all of those individuals who are affected by the existing problematic situation. Some individuals will be favorably affected by the status quo institutional regime, while others will be bearing unwanted costs of the status quo ante. If policy reform is to succeed it will be necessary for those who are currently bearing unwanted costs to make a political commitment to join in efforts to alter the institutional regime. If successful, these individuals will emerge as "winners" while others will be considered "losers." This is unfortunate since it will tend to harden opposition to important policy changes that will, perhaps, hold profoundly important gains for society as a whole.

Effective policy reform requires the creation of a political consensus that can make the case for institutional change. Smart policy reforms are those that focus on existing economic incentives, constraints, and habituated practices. It is these aspects of an economy that inform individual action, and it is from these practices that adjustments will be required. It is best if these individuals, so central to problematic behavior, play an active role in careful analyses of current policies, and the problems to which those policies give rise. These individuals must then, if possible, also participate in the quest for new and feasible policy options and strategies for implementation. Also, successful policy reforms must be clear about the steps for achieving effective compliance.

An additional advantage of engaging key interested parties is that if the first round of reforms fails to address the policy problem in its entirety, those who had been engaged might be called upon to help refine and revise earlier reforms. On the other hand, if policy reform is top-down in nature, it is likely that important parties will be excluded and will then be potential impediments at the implementation stage. While consultation with all key parties is integral to successful policy dialogue, unanimous support is not required for all reform; some accommodations can be made for some affected groups if this will help to get reforms moving in the right direction.

Engage them in the process

Policy reform requires effective leadership at each stage of the process. This means that all interested parties must be enlisted as participants in the process. As above, some of those interested parties will see themselves as "losers" in the process, while others will quickly learn that they might gain some important advantages from policy reform. These latter individuals and groups are the likely places to find *policy entrepreneurs*. They are more than mere "champions" of policy reform. Effective policy reforms require individuals to help bridge the gap between those who are comfortable and satisfied with the status quo institutional setup, and those who are currently disadvantaged—whether by perverse incentives, by destructive pollution, or by impediments to their improved livelihoods. Policy entrepreneurs might be in national or local government bodies, NGOs, or various interest groups.

It is unavoidable that policy reform will be contentious. And it is therefore unlikely that one or a few policy entrepreneurs will be able to satisfy all of the contending interests. But to expect this is to place too much emphasis on a few key players. Policy reforms must be advanced as necessary solutions to a set of problems that affect many people—and in that sense policy entrepreneurs have the more important job of explaining their urgency to a conflicted public. In a practical sense, "good" policy reforms are those that can be adopted by a skeptical audience of policy makers and citizens. That is, if reforms advocated by a group of "experts" cannot gain traction in a democratic political structure, perhaps the reforms are not very "good."

Promote local ownership

As we see above, policy reform asks certain interest groups in an economy to suspend disbelief and to go along with new ideas about how to organize social and economic relations. The one sure thing we know about humans is that we are afraid of change—unless it is change that we ourselves initiate. By bringing many diverse interests into the discussion of policy reform—drawn from promoters and opponents—the odds are increased that "ownership" of the final result will be enhanced and spread more widely. This is essential for policy reform to succeed.

It is essential to keep in mind that early success in policy reform does not necessarily ensure sustainability in modified policy outcomes. The policy-reform process entails incremental changes in ideas, in visions, in goals, and in objectives of diverse and widely scattered individual interests. To support and facilitate such a process, individual governments and donors must make a long-term commitment to work with and sustain the entities that participate in policy formulation and implementation. Donors must develop comprehensive and integrated plans and programs employing a range of targeted delivery mechanisms to anticipate and address barriers to policy reform. Periodic assessment of progress is essential to the judicious use of financial resources and to make adjustments in the assistance program.

It must be kept in mind that policy reform is always underway. New scarcities emerge, new relative prices suggest certain other problems, new technology calls our attention to unforeseen issues, and so a democratic market economy is always in the process of becoming. From this it follows that economic policies must constantly be modified and updated. Exquisite policy analysis and dialogue must be sustained throughout the policy process. This enduring engagement builds collaborative relationships that will last long after any particular reform has been completed. Donors must carefully evaluate political, economic, and social circumstances as a precursor to recommending policy reform. Enduring political and cultural traditions influence government receptiveness to new policy proposals. Outside advisors, although well prepared and bringing good intentions, cannot assess all of these circumstances. A careful and considered approach meets with greater receptivity—and thus increased likelihood of success.

Engage other donors

One enduring challenge confronting meaningful policy reform is that several donors are usually at work in a given country—most of them working on separate problems. At times it can seem that these independent efforts to be helpful can actually make matters worse. Often, these separate activities are predicated on vastly different assumptions, development goals, and approaches. If those differences are to be worked out in the best interest of the host country then it will require that donor dialogue must have greater coordination and consideration of these differences.

This would suggest that for large-scale policy reforms, donors must unite around a single approach and reform strategy. Unfortunately, as alluded to above, the policy priorities and organizational imperatives of various donors often make this integrated approach difficult. A donor's willingness to fund particular policy reforms may be tied to the adoption of a specific institutional change that happens to be in vogue at the time. Advocacy of various micro-finance programs has certainly had this effect. This pre-commitment to a few solutions can inhibit openness—and it often pre-empts national or local leadership in the reform process. More seriously, when donors have different visions of the appropriate reform goals and strategies, resulting pressures on host-country policy makers are generally counterproductive. The need for donor coordination is further heightened by the importance of policy consistency across sectors. For reasons of efficiency and national priorities, donors may allocate priority sectors among themselves, with one donor taking the lead in the health sector and another in agriculture. However, it is best if policy measures across all sectors are linked by the underlying principles on which the policies are based.

Both donors and host governments will usually have durable practices (habits) that harm prospects for enhanced coordination. One particularly unwelcome practice is the project-driven approach to development assistance. A consistent focus on donor-driven projects can easily prevent the emergence of durable collaborative relationships among donors. In fairness to donors, we must admit that many governments prefer to deal with each donor separately. That is, countries can sometimes play one donor off against others in a perverse game that benefits no one.

Foster communications

Create a climate of open communication

As the above discussion makes clear, policy reform is contentious. Every economic interest wishes to have its current situation advanced or protected. It cannot be a surprise that the politics of policy reform is a serious endeavor. The best possible protection from accusations of favoritism is complete openness—transparency—of the entire process. And transparency cannot be seen as a passive characteristic of policy reform. Transparency implies active promotion of information dissemination, and of discussions about the information that is made available. Donors and governments do not have a monopoly on good ideas. Open communication serves to legitimize the often-difficult choices required when policy reform gets underway.

The idea of open communication must not be understood as a few vested interests interacting with a monolithic government. Effective communication requires that a variety of pertinent government agencies communicate among themselves, as well as with a variety of pertinent interests. Again, easily understood information on the nature of reforms—and progress in their implementation—will help to legitimize the policy-reform process among the general public.

Transparency concerns both the openness and the accountability of the process of policy reform. Transparency and accountability are mutually reinforcing—the more transparent the flow of information, the easier is the task of accounting for and enhancing the perceived legitimacy of the reforms. However, for individual interested parties (and the general public) to use this information effectively, there must be provisions for access to the policy process including involvement in dialogue, public hearings, and opportunities to provide written and oral comments on policies throughout the process. Of course some participants will always seek to provide—or rely upon—information that only supports their positions. NGOs and trade associations can play a role in monitoring government on behalf of these groups, by conducting independent assessments of policy performance, and by educating their members so they can effectively confront their officials, raise these issues, and hold government accountable.

Develop a shared understanding of the problem

We have repeatedly stressed the importance of clarity regarding the nature of existing policy problems, and of the emerging solutions to those problems. Information and supporting data concerning policy problems must be collected, processed, and communicated to the general public in a way that will underwrite informed and evidence-based discussions. This information can then be used to create a shared understanding of the current policy problems and possible solutions.

Government ministries are often required to provide certain information to the general public, and to respond to requests for information. In addition, there is a considerable amount of information collected, processed, and communicated informally. The effective use of this information will help to create consensus about pressing policy problems and will facilitate the policy-reform process. The context for building this shared understanding involves a range of interrelated factors: (1) What, exactly, are the policy problems requiring attention? (2) What do these existing policies and their outcomes suggest in terms of changes in the behavior of individuals, groups, and particular industries? (3) Who are the probable winners and losers? (4) How did the policy and the problems it creates come into existence—is it the result of government-initiated analyses or were changes tied to pressures from donors and others? While the policy process provides the primary context for the collection of information, information systems must also respond to a variety of interrelated and changeable factors such as fiscal and monetary conditions, the political situation, and social and cultural settings.

It is quite common to find that information collection and analysis is under-funded and under-appreciated. Often this will be the result of the lack of demo-cratic (participatory) political processes. It is always the case that because information is costly to collect and utilize, care must be exercised to make sure that the most informative data receives the greatest attention. In some societies without a tradition of participation in policy reform, even greater care is called for. This greater caution is necessary because in such societies it will be too easy to dismiss data collection and dissemination as frivolous expenses.

Assess progress to enhance learning and adaptation

We have already stressed the importance of an open and flexible dialogue about policy reform. As above, effective involvement requires donor familiarity with the specific political, economic, and cultural contexts within which policy reform will occur. Such knowledge can be gained by forging respectful partnerships and alli-ances with key members of local organizations and other independent experts.

With that relationship in place, donors can strengthen these partnerships and processes of policy dialogue. By sharing and learning about appropriate assessment, analytical, and diagnostic activities, donors can play a more effective role in this process of reform. Donors must engage key individuals and groups to enhance the policy process. Learning and adaptation are the essential aspects of successful reforms. The usual turnover in political leadership—and thus centers of influence—means that it is prudent to engage diverse constituencies throughout the process. Recall that policy reform creates "winners" and "losers" by changing the status quo. Hence, an important component to any dialogue is structuring it to anticipate and address the concerns and perceptions of the losers and finding ways to get them to support the reform process.

Changes in the political, economic, or cultural contexts can lead to important changes in the nature and scope of the policy dialogue. Changes in economic fac-tors such as market prices, new products (e.g. corn or oil palm used for biofuels) from natural resources, or changes in inflation or exchange rates, profoundly alter the value of land and related resources, and in the process also change the level of interest in the process of policy reform. All participants in the policy dialogue, from donors to donor partners, must understand how these changes affect the climate for policy reform. Policy reforms, even though modest, entail costs as well as benefits, which change the social and economic context. Since some parties and individuals may benefit more than others, it is important to keep the policy dialogue as trans-parent as possible and to keep open lines of communication. This will enhance learning and adaptation.

It may be useful to organize structured dialogue—round-table discussions—with governmental officials. Another possibility would be exchange programs among countries so that policy makers and key interested individuals can see similar situations in which policy reforms have altered the decision environment for individuals and firms. Cooperation with local universities and policy analysis institutes that advise key government decision makers can benefit the process of policy reform. This interaction may occur as part of training courses and other settings. Local communities and NGOs can contribute important insights and leadership to policy dialogue.

It is common for donors to offer assistance in strengthening local government bodies and institutes. These entities can be highly effective and credible agents of policy reform. For example, they can carry out studies that bear on policy issues, and if they have done sound work, local policy makers and key interest groups will have an easier time extending trust and credibility.

Communicate successes and setbacks

There can be strong pressures for donors to be protective of their role in policymaking. It is politically awkward to claim much credit for policy-reform success, and it is even worse to admit responsibility for policy-reform failures. But failure is different from setbacks, and it can be extremely useful if donors adopt a stance of modesty concerning successes, and honesty concerning setbacks. Donors must be seen as contributing to policy reform without being seen as the reason for successful reforms. This necessary visibility reinforces the idea that donors are important partners in the process—and it reminds all participants that desired improvements in economic and social outcomes are the joint product of donor assistance and host government commitments. There will always be setbacks in policy reform, and yet the long-run prospects of continued success in such efforts will depend on the willingness of host governments and donors to acknowledge setbacks. More important, governments and donors must show themselves to be dedicated to the diagnosis of those setbacks. As we have stressed, policy reform is a continual activity in which "adaptive management" is the operative metaphor. Openness and honesty about setbacks is the launching pad for future enduring successes.

As stewards of the economy, governments are accountable for decisions that contribute to economic coherence and perhaps growth. Policies (institutions) comprise the "rules of the game" for members of the economy from households to multinational corporations. Governments are justifiably concerned about compromising their sovereignty if new institutional arrangements seem to emerge from excessive donor influence. Domestic policy makers must maintain their credibility both within their own government but especially among those affected by their policies. This credibility is easily undermined if donors are perceived to be leading rather than supporting policy reform and implementation.

It is expected that policy reform will encounter bureaucratic resistance. Established protocols for revising legislation and regulations must be respected, even if this renders the process slow and uncertain. Government officials may sometimes seek to slow down certain reforms because of opposition from within the government—but especially from within the ministry that will be responsible for implementation.

It is therefore to be expected that policy reform activities may be less welcome than standard bricks-and-mortar activities. The obvious danger, however, is that even bricks-and-mortar projects, if not accompanied by the appropriate policy environment, are unsustainable.

We stress that the inevitable setbacks in policy reform must not be allowed to undermine the need to persist with solving difficult policy problems. Setbacks or discouraging results along the way offer important learning opportunities and a chance to adapt approaches—and even the goals—of policy reform. It is important that "the best not be the enemy of the better." Often it is wise for donors to take the successes that can be achieved, and to return to the more difficult problems at a later time. As we have stressed repeatedly, policy reform must be seen as a continual process of refining the working rules of the economy.

Create confidence

Build trust among participants

The most effective reforms emerge in response to locally recognized interests, needs, and priorities. An essential component of successful policy reform is a climate of shared trust among all participants. While natural disasters or large-scale human-caused events can create an immediate interest in institutional change, it is more common to find that institutional change must be motivated by policy entrepreneurs. In such cases, trust is essential.

Particular windows of opportunity increase the commitment of policy makers and interested parties to policy reform and thereby enhance the chances of successful reforms. Events that may create these opportunities include media exposure of a high-profile economic crisis, a man-made calamity, or a natural disaster. Changes of government or of senior personnel within government—whether local, regional, or national—can provide new opportunities for launching a much-needed policy dialogue. These changes often correspond with a shift in relationships among interest groups that can remove or greatly modify previous barriers to policy change. At times of such change, building and maintaining trust is an important component of successful policy reform.

It is much easier for donors to take advantage of opportunities for policy reform if they have previously established high levels of trust with host governments. It is important to recognize that being at the right place at the right time is more than luck. It is being prepared. Other windows of opportunity can result from a confluence of changes. In one instance (Indonesia), a sudden change in the long-standing, highly centralized Suharto regime led to sudden and radical decentralization and opportunities to work directly on locally determined economic development strategies and plans. Those donors who had long been pressing for greater local participation in development planning, and who had developed relationships of trust with local governments and NGOs, were able to take advantage of this quick change.

Develop good analytical skills

Given the highly contentious nature of policy reform, problem definition and diagnosis must be grounded on the very best analytical methods. Good analysis can help to explain and justify necessary policy reforms. Certain reforms depend on a society's broader economic, political, and governance conditions. The integrative perspective of economics focuses on trade-offs between externalities, resource management, and demands for conventional goods and services. Market failures result when prices reflect only private costs, ignoring the significant public costs to society or the economy. A lack of effective regulatory monitoring or enforcement capacity permits producers and consumers to neglect the potential, external social and economic impacts of production, consumption, and other activities. An integrated policy perspective will include an examination of taxes, regulations, and other policy instruments that a government can apply to rectify economic externalities (market failures).

While externalities are often pervasive in developing countries, excessive pollution and resource depletion will also result from distortion of market forces, scarce human capital, and weak institutional underpinnings of a market economy. Policy reform can address such policy failures by focusing on increased awareness of flawed incentives in the realms of both production and consumption. Opportunities exist to increase efficiency, promote equity, and conserve natural resources through appropriate pricing and cost recovery. For example, higher prices (or reduced subsidies) can induce water users (both consumers and irrigation farmers) to use water more judiciously. Micro-level incentives must reflect the macro-level options available. For example, if a policy change aims to slow the rate of agricultural expansion into forested lands, it will not be sufficient to formulate a new regulation prohibiting deforestation. Rather, macroeconomic policies must be revised to encourage alternative income sources for farm households. Access to fertilizer and credit, market infrastructure, imported or domestic availability of agricultural machinery, and foreign exchange policies may have as much influence on deforestation rates as forestry sector policies.

Today's major global and local policy issues—global climate change, trade liberalization, product sanitary and phyto-sanitary standards, unsustainable land use, natural resource depletion, air and water pollution, the demographic resource imbalance—all require action that cuts across national, sector, and organizational boundaries. High-quality analysis enhances the chances for meaningful debates on these and other issues.

Use best practices

The policy process is too often perceived as linear, top-down, and inflexible. Where countries do not have a long tradition of public participation in policy debates, this can indeed be the case. In such settings, policy reform is liable to be derailed by conflict and delay.

The reform process can move forward, and the policy dialogue can advance, only if the venues, processes, and means employed in that dialogue are the best possible instruments of reaching agreement on the nature and extent of current policy problems, and of plausible resolution of those problems. Open and candid dialogue is the key to successful policy reform. The plausible components of this dialogue can include formal hearings, facilitated negotiations, informal meetings, observational study tours, workshops, conferences, and more recently, the use of electronic forms of dialogue (list serves, web pages, chat rooms, etc.). The policy dialogue should engage a variety of activities so that a variety of perspectives is captured and incorporated into the decision process.

Different issues are best handled in different ways. The challenge is to select the best form of policy dialogue for the particular issues under discussion. Public hearings and "listening sessions" can be effective instruments early in the process. As problem definition progresses, some degree of feedback and calibration will suggest more structured settings. Factors to take into consideration include the type of venue, who should organize the dialogue activity, whether there is a need for professional facilitation, and who should participate. The answers to these questions will depend on the nature of the policy problem under consideration, as well as anticipated obstacles and opportunities that emerge during the process.

The success of policy reform will depend on who organizes and facilitates the dialogue and related activities. As noted elsewhere, all policy (institutional) reform inevitably creates the perception that some individuals and groups will be "winners" while other individuals and groups will be "losers." This suggests that efforts will be required to prevent the process getting stuck at the outset—or becoming locked into rather standard conflictual circumstances. One useful device is to employ the services of a neutral "outside" party (or parties). Examples of such facilitators include university researchers, professional staff of a university institute, an NGO, or even another donor who may be positioned to host meetings or workshops. Policy reforms often involve approaches or policy instruments that are new to the host country, but for which there is considerable international experience. Study tours to engage host-country policy makers can enrich the policy dialogue and may provide an appropriate forum for sharing international experience and anticipating problematic issues in the immediate context.

Policy reform often entails innovative analytical approaches, and new conceptual understandings (e.g. a carbon tax, contingent valuation approaches). To improve the effectiveness of the entire process, it will be necessary to carry out certain preparatory activities to make sure the approaches fit the local context. This early work will focus on data availability, conformity of the technique with local cultural norms, and the credibility with which the findings of such approaches might be judged. Such preparation will help to focus discussions and will help to anticipate potentially controversial issues.

Draw on early successes to bolster confidence

One of the major impediments in policy reform is a sense that local policy makers and ministry staff are not quite up to the challenge. This unfortunate belief is often unjustified, but it persists and it can undermine feasible progress. Donors will need to take extra effort to instill confidence in all participants in the policy-reform process. This capacity-building will be enhanced if the process is designed so that early success is achieved, and if it is clear that these small steps are a prelude to more complex activities as the process moves forward.

Policy reform often involves the introduction of management approaches or analytical tools that have not previously been employed in the host country. These approaches may necessitate the recruitment of specialized staff—and training for both existing and new staff. Capacity building entails the design of good training plans to enhance effectiveness of reforms. Doing so is important for gaining and sustaining momentum. Momentum is important as the reform process approaches implementation. It is here that the reform process will often encounter weak capacity—both individually and organizationally. Issues that may account for weak capacity include limited access to information or skills to evaluate alternatives, and to select the best ways forward.

Implications

Our discussion of managing the policy process is intended to offer explicit and practical guidance to development practitioners around the globe. Our lessons are drawn from several decades of lessons learned and best practices from a wide range of projects and programs undertaken by the U.S. Agency for International Development, the World Bank, the regional development banks, and various donors. The emphasis here has been on the ideal ways to interact with others in the donor community—but especially with host-country counterparts—to make sure that the contestations and inherent difficulties of policy reform cannot sidetrack much-needed reforms.

We now turn to the equally difficult challenge of how best to actually carry out policy reform. We call it "working with the policy-reform process."

8

WORKING WITH THE POLICY-REFORM PROCESS

> All reason functions *within* traditions.
>
> (Richard Bernstein 1983: 130)

As we saw in Chapter 7, there are five essential activities that comprise the policy-reform process. These are: (1) problem diagnosis; (2) policy design; (3) implementation of new policies; (4) adaptation; and (5) evaluating outcomes (see Table 8.1).

Diagnose policy problems

Document the negative impacts and incidence of current situation

Specific social and economic problems are the predictable results (symptoms) of specific institutional arrangements in the economy. As our discussion in Chapters 5 and 6 makes clear, outcomes follow from institutions. Economic problems are not simply random events—they have their reasons and their causes. The first job of those who wish to undertake policy reform is to follow the causal trail from problems (results or symptoms) back to their reasons or causes. That is the essence of abduction.

When citizens and political leaders identify a new problem in need of correction, they are also acknowledging that certain underlying institutional arrangements (existing policies) are implicated in that expression of dissatisfaction. In short, the institutional arrangements, perhaps thought to be reasonable when they were first adopted, are no longer recognized as benign. But of course what seems reasonable to one group of citizens will not necessarily seem reasonable to others. This brings us to the difficult problem of "winners" and "losers" in an existing policy setting.

TABLE 8.1 Best practices for working with the policy-reform process

	Best practices
Diagnose policy problems (**Explaining**)	1. Document negative impacts and incidence of current situation.
	2. Conduct analyses of the political and economic reasons for the problem.
Design policy solutions (**Creating**)	3. Develop policy options to solve existing policy problems.
	4. Create feasible implementation strategies.
Implement new policies (**Changing**)	5. Assess current organizational roles and capacities for change.
	6. Document incentives facing interested parties.
Facilitate adaptation (**Complying**)	7. Assure that policy solutions are sustainable.
	8. Delegate responsibility.
Evaluate outcomes (**Judging**)	9. Monitor and assess compliance with new policies.
	10. Assess new policy outcomes to judge if success or failure.

The identification of winners and losers can also be thought of in terms of certain individuals or groups being *advantaged* by particular policy outcomes and their underlying institutional causes, while others are *disadvantaged* by those same outcomes. Policy reform inevitably implies that those individuals and groups currently enjoying particular advantages are likely to see themselves as losers from policy reform. Similarly, those currently harmed (disadvantaged) by prevailing policy outcomes expect to be winners in policy reform.

If agricultural chemicals are now creating serious problems for artisanal fishers then it is obvious who is currently advantaged and who is disadvantaged. Policy reform to resolve this situation will likely be characterized as the fishing community winning while farmers are the losers. Successful policy reform must seek to reduce the impacts on those who perceive themselves as losing their current advantage in the status quo. The fundamental task of diagnosis is to analyze the reasons why certain unwanted outcomes persist. An essential aspect of this process of diagnosis is to be clear about who the winners and losers are in the current situation. This information on current advantages and disadvantages will then help direct analytical attention to the existing policies (institutions) that produce those outcomes. If agricultural pesticides are subsidized by the government, and if there are no laws (policies) concerning application rates of those pesticides, then it cannot be a surprise why artisanal fishermen are the victims of pollution.

Some policies enjoy wide popular support and therefore it is difficult to identify clear winners and losers. But such policies may carry serious problems for the economy and undermine its overall effectiveness. An example of this might be free (or deeply subsidized) electricity that deprives the electricity sector of the accountability and funding it requires in order to undertake proper maintenance and investment.

Analysis of the incidence of advantage and disadvantage in the current policy setting must be carefully documented. Policy reform is most successful when it is motivated by evidenced-based analysis. If lead is thought to be harming children then it is essential that those claims be documented with plausible evidence. If agricultural productivity is thought to be harmed by the absence of good extension programs then that case must be made with evidence that will withstand scrutiny. If corruption is thought to undermine foreign investment then evidence to that effect must be marshaled and made available.

Plausible diagnosis requires clarity about the connection between policies and outcomes. In a market economy, individuals respond to signals from the market and those signals become incentives to act in particular ways. The explanation for unwanted outcomes runs backwards to the incentives that individuals face as they go about their daily lives. And if we then follow that causal chain back another step we will encounter specific policies that will comprise the reasons for—the explanation of—the unwanted outcomes. Diagnosis of important policy problems will inevitably encounter hostility and opposition from those who might be disadvantaged by possible reforms. Analysis of the effects and incidence of the status quo—and plausible policy alternatives—must be carefully carried out and well documented. Mistakes at this stage will undermine all reform prospects. The analysis must be subjected to careful review by a range of interested parties. They may not like the findings, but they must accept the underlying analytical protocols, and the data employed.

Conduct analyses of the political and economic reasons for the problem

Accurate and comprehensive problem diagnosis is essential if there is to emerge a clear understanding of the political and economic reasons for existing unacceptable policy outcomes. This analysis must be carried out and reported in terms that will hold meaning for all interest groups. It must stand up to careful scrutiny by various interest groups who will see policy reform as a threat to their existing political and economic circumstances. The credibility of the reform process depends on the care and thoroughness with which this analysis is carried out.

Successful policy reform is impossible without reliable analysis concerning why the problem exists. The analysis of why specific policy problems persist will represent a threat to those individuals and groups currently enjoying an economic advantage. These individuals can be expected to resist reforms that will harm their economic situation. Involving local experts is a good strategy on two counts. First, local knowledge always enriches and lends essential detail to analysis carried out by foreign experts. Second, the very fact of having local expertise contributing to the analysis will add credibility. Of course not all local experts are objective or knowledgeable so some caution is called for. But engaging local experts will often bolster credibility.

If careless analysis is carried out the entire policy-reform process will be in jeopardy. With adequate funding it will be easier to gain the collaboration of other donor partners—thereby adding credibility to this important activity. Important insights can often be gained by drawing on analyses and experiences with similar situations in other circumstances. Other countries may have dealt with a similar problem, or they may have developed promising diagnostic protocols. Care is required when relying on a single academic discipline for an assessment of the policy problem. Each discipline has a tendency to define problems in its own terms—thereby implying that only its practitioners are capable of designing policies to correct the problem. If possible, several perspectives and analytical approaches should be sought. This will allow a number of facets of the policy problem to be considered.

Design policy solutions

Develop policy options

It is rare to find a single policy solution to an existing policy problem. Therefore, the policy-reform process works best if problem diagnosis leads directly into the creation of several feasible policy options. It is important to understand that the concept of an "ideal policy option" does not exist in isolation from consideration of the eventual adoption of that policy. Policy reform is not an activity in pursuit of the optimal policy as imagined in the eyes of donors or outside disciplinary experts. Rather, policy reform is a process of working with all relevant interested parties to find an acceptable solution to an existing policy setting that is no longer acceptable.

Experience shows that the "best" design can fail unless the realities of implementation are anticipated and addressed before the final design is agreed upon. An inclusive and participatory process must be used throughout the diagnosis phase. Moreover, those who will play an eventual role in actual implementation—agency and ministry officials—must be engaged in the process of diagnosis and policy design. Once a policy has been agreed upon, various branches of government still may possess the ability to derail policy implementation. Certain officials, even if they are not directly involved in implementation, can undermine new policy initiatives through the way they allocate budgets to implementing ministries, by how the law and regulations are specified, and by the technical guidance that will emerge to enforce new policies.

In some countries, courts can impede implementation by enjoining new legislation and administrative rules. Policy reforms that include enforcement sanctions as a deterrent to noncompliance will depend on the support of the judicial branch of government to define the parameters of enforcement, to prosecute violations, and to levy sanctions commensurate with the violation. In many countries it can be difficult to prosecute the poor. At the other end, prosecuting the politically and economically powerful is equally difficult. New policies must be crafted with great attention to enforceability. Unfortunately, the practice is often just the opposite—strict and far-reaching new rules are passed that have little prospect for enforcement and compliance. It appears as if problems have been addressed when in fact nothing actually changes.

Following legislative approval, responsibility for implementation usually shifts to government ministries. Problems can arise if there has been unclear delineation of roles and responsibilities, if there are few financial resources or limited administrative capacity to carry out the new responsibilities, or if there is a lack of commitment to the new policy on the part of the implementing ministry. This problem will be worsened if the new policies have been the exclusive province of a small group of policy elites in distant capitals. Those individuals and groups that are the possible beneficiaries of policy reform are often not in a political or economic position to assert their interests in policy reforms. The balance can sometimes be shifted in their favor by a public-relations effort that will explain the reasons for the reforms to the larger public. It is here that NGOs can play a valuable role.

As mentioned earlier, potential implementation barriers must be evaluated and planned for during the diagnostic phase. This means that potential implementing ministries and interested parties must be involved from the beginning. It is here that certain "ideal" policies will need to be re-formulated to accommodate likely implementation hurdles. As we suggested earlier, a policy cannot, by definition, be ideal if it cannot be implemented.

Create feasible implementation strategies

An ideal implementation strategy is one that follows the general principles of adaptive management. That is, the approach should be carefully specified at the outset, and yet it must be capable of adjustment as the process moves forward. Clear implementation plans alert all participants as to what steps will be followed, and what specific roles will be played by various individuals. But these detailed plans must also indicate the potential for flexibility in the face of unexpected obstacles as the process moves forward. Detailed plans should offer a compliance schedule, and they should help implementers identify key gaps as the process advances. With a careful implementation plan, donors will be able to target their financial and programmatic assistance effectively. And good implementation plans help local and national governments understand the importance of being clear about the cause-and-effect structure of policy reform.

The design stage of policy reform is often one of intense last-minute negotiations, fine-tuning of new laws, and mobilization of political (and also legislative) support. Practical issues relating to implementation budgets, compliance planning, and capacity building are put aside to concentrate efforts on approval of the policy. Once the policy is approved, stewardship for the new policy (or policies) shifts to implementing agencies and ministries. Implementation is much enhanced if the momentum from earlier stages can be maintained into the often-difficult phase of implementing the new institutional and organizational arrangements that define the nature and extent of complete policy reform.

One of the major difficulties during implementation is the provision of necessary inducements and incentives for those public servants who are expected to carry the burden of bringing the new reforms to effective fruition. Often, understaffing leads to overworked staff and this can delay progress, as well as develop into resistance to planned changes. Care must be taken to make sure that there are incentives in place to help staff adjust to the new policy regime. Most donors are prohibited from compensating government staff for the time they spend on coordination of donor projects. In some countries ministry staff may receive salary supplements when they participate in donor-financed activities such as training, workshops, and advisory or steering committees. Such incentives can lead staff to pursue these financial rewards to the exclusion of other work. In some cases, training and study tours to other countries can partially compensate for lower salaries. Ultimately, issues of staff incentives and high salary differentials can be addressed only through comprehensive civil service reforms. This suggests that donors can collaborate with ministries to make sure that staff training and study tours are concentrated in those areas where the need for policy reform is greatest. If staff members have previously been exposed to the policy reform process, successful implementation is more likely.

The public can be an important ally of civil servants in their implementation efforts, but for this to work it is necessary that the public have access to essential information, and that there is an opportunity to participate in the review and oversight of implementation actions. This will be extremely important in those instances where the "losers" of planned policy reform are in a position to block certain actions. Bilateral assistance programs often feature democratization as a key objective, offering significant opportunities for changing the nature of public–private relationships. By conducting implementation activities openly and transparently, and by providing public access to information on economic performance to assist monitoring and enforcement, governments can demonstrate their commitment to accountability, and they can legitimize their new enforcement role with interested parties.

Implement new policies

Assess organizational roles and capacities

The process of policy reform has two central dimensions—one concerning ideas about problems and their solution, the other concerning changes in individual behavior in response to the acknowledgment that the status quo is giving rise to unacceptable outcomes. Much discussion focuses on the interests of particular groups in society that we have referred to as potential "winners" and "losers." But it must be understood that there will often be much resistance to change inside of government agencies whose employees have grown accustomed to a particular style of work, and to the comfort of interacting with their specialized constituencies. Serious implementation hurdles will not be restricted to important political and economic actors but may also thrive inside of government.

A number of factors can impede the implementation of new policy as it was originally designed. Before implementation assistance is provided, it is necessary to analyze the policy in terms of likely barriers to implementation, and to identify those factors that may reduce its effectiveness once implemented. These assessments will help to overcome barriers and other impediments. This is especially important when the donor has not been involved in earlier stages of the policy reform process, or donor support is requested for implementation of an existing policy. The assessment may indicate the need for changes in the policy or in the implementation strategy.

Donors are often asked to provide assistance with the implementation of new policies. This may involve training for staff in ministries or technical assistance for prominent interest groups. Possible reasons for difficulty in implementation can include: (1) standard bureaucratic weaknesses in organizational capacity; (2) the inability of affected parties to respond to incentives because of their limited financial situation; or (3) poor information. The scope of assessment will depend on the nature and timing of the request for assistance, as well as the resources the donor can mobilize for the assessment. At one extreme, the scope of assessment may be quite broad and take several months to complete. Where the request for assistance focuses on a single policy reform, the scope of analysis may be limited.

If there is agreement that a new or revised policy is flawed, the obvious next step is to determine whether the policy can be revised. Donors and their assistance partners must examine the design process, determine how long it took to approve the policy, understand the major issues that had to be overcome before consensus was reached, and assess the receptiveness of policy makers to changes in the original policy. If the policy has been in place for several years, changes are likely to entail a comprehensive assessment and vetting of this analysis at the stage of problem diagnosis. Again, if donors have participated in the design process, the prospects for changing the policy prior to implementation may be greater.

As a rule, it is easier to address flaws in policy design during the implementation stage if those flaws relate to the organizational capacity of implementers and affected parties, rather than to poorly designed incentive structures. However, even if the ultimate success of implementation is uncertain, donor efforts to support reform may enhance its credibility and commitment to assisting the partner, and perhaps provide an opportunity to revise the policy at some future date.

Document incentives facing interested parties

It is important to assess the structure of existing incentives and the factors that may reduce a new policy's effectiveness. Ideally, new institutional arrangements will result in certain and predictable directional changes in individual choice and action. Flaws in the design of new institutional arrangements (new rules), or weak implementation will most certainly undermine the goals and objectives of the policy process. Some of these issues can be anticipated and corrected at the design stage, while others will require adjustments during implementation to overcome design flaws.

Policy reforms alter the incentive structure of firms and individuals by compelling behavioral changes, or by establishing new prices for inputs, outputs, or pollution that will induce new behaviors. For some policy issues, altered rules giving rise to new incentives may be adequate to bring about new behaviors. In other settings, the new rules may actually compel new behaviors. Designers of policies must be aware of uncertain macroeconomic and market conditions that make it difficult to predict how and when firms and individuals will respond to policy changes.

Trade policies, general fiscal policies, and sector policies must be considered when attempting to predict the individual responses to sanctions and incentives embedded in new policies. Those who design new policies will need to be aware of these confounding influences. The presumption of policy reform is that, overall, the beneficial impacts will be positive. But of course some interest groups may well lose some economic advantage. The incidence of gains and losses from policy reform will engender some degree of political concern and perhaps opposition. Some key characteristics of this structure of benefits and costs must be recognized in formulating policy. First, most new policies benefit a relatively large group for which benefits per beneficiary are small. On the other hand, the financial and other costs of new policies can sometimes fall disproportionately on particular individuals, groups, industries or facilities. Second, benefits from some policy reforms may occur quickly. However, in other instances, benefits may not be fully realized for several years, while the costs often occur rather soon. In other words, benefits may not occur until the affected industry has had a chance to respond with investment in new technology, resources or trained labor. Third, beneficial impacts arising from policy reforms are often indirectly related to the affected industry or economic sector (e.g. resulting in cleaner water and air, reduced soil erosion or deforestation). On the other hand, the costs of policy reforms can be both direct (i.e. the cost to business) and indirect (i.e. cost to society and the economy from structural changes in consumption, production and employment). Fourth, powerful stakeholders can be expected to exert pressure in the reform process to alter incentive structures in their favor, dilute enforcement, or derail the policy entirely. Finally, those interested parties that will be affected negatively by a policy outcome are often better organized than those likely to benefit from change because the beneficiaries of policy reform are often the public at large. In such cases, the incidence of transaction costs makes it most unlikely that widely scattered beneficiaries will be able to offset the highly concentrated incidence of the potential losers of policy reform.

Facilitate adaptation

Assure that policy solutions are sustainable

Donor financing is often key during the start-up phase of policy implementation, but it may hinder the development of domestic funding if support is viewed as a permanent substitute for a strong commitment from government to support financing when the donor funding phases out. Sustained financing is not limited to expenditures by implementing ministries. Governments are not expected to shoulder the responsibility for financing in the private or municipal sector, but they can play an important role in creating new laws and rules, and adopting and enforcing policies that will solidify the commitment of all affected parties.

Some central authorities have delegated responsibility for various aspects of national economic management and governance to local governments, community-based organizations (CBOs), or occasionally NGOs. Decentralization may be motivated by a desire to reduce demands on central budgets, or it may be recognition of the comparative political and/or performance advantages of local management. In many instances, however, when transfer of these responsibilities has not been accompanied by funding to cover costs or authorization to implement revenue mechanisms, an unfunded mandate has been created. As donor support is withdrawn, other sources such as local governments, NGOs, or private voluntary organizations (PVOs), may be inadequate to cover all management costs.

Donors often provide assistance in financing or co-financing infrastructure investments or equipment related to public services (e.g. garbage trucks or trash compactors) or management needs (e.g. computers and other office or technical equipment). Investment financing is often more attractive to donors than support for recurring operational costs since the benefits are immediate and easier to quantify. In addition, "tied" aid support provides opportunities for vendors in the donor country to enter the market in the recipient country. The benefits of these investments will be diminished without a commitment to fund recurring operational costs such as maintenance, spare parts, fuel and electricity, staff and training. Part of the reason for unsustainable financing can be traced to the design of donor programs. Project assistance often is not contingent on financial contributions from the recipients. More recently, donors have gained a greater appreciation for the use of counterpart incentives, "graduation" provisions, matching funding, public–private partnerships, and diversifying assistance to help partners develop their own financing to sustain projects and programs over the long term.

Delegate responsibility

Local actors often can implement changes in the most cost-effective and sustainable manner. Local incentives are the driving force for widespread adoption of improved methods, and removing policy obstacles to sound investment systematically helps to improve incentives. Delegating implementation responsibility to those who are close to the problem can very often improve effectiveness because these local parties tend to be more motivated to carry out policies as designed, regularly monitor compliance, and have greater credibility and accountability with affected parties.

Throughout the developing world, donors have encouraged the decentralization of many of the functions of government. In part, this strategy has been motivated by a political agenda to democratize government, spread power more widely, and lay the foundation for greater participation in the election process. These changes are motivated by concerns over whether national policies are always best implemented by central authorities. In case after case, devolving responsibilities to local authorities has often increased the effectiveness of policy implementation.

Central ministries often contribute to the implementation effort, taking a lead role in interpreting legislation by writing regulations or more informal procedures. Central ministries also may be better positioned to secure financing needed at the local level, resolve disputes, and monitor and evaluate the effectiveness of implementation. Local roles in implementation usually involve direct contact with affected parties in such activities as development and review of permits, monitoring and review of compliance activities, and enforcement.

Evaluate outcomes

Monitor and assess compliance with new policies

The process of evaluation must be tailored to answer the set of questions that donors, their partners, and other donor partners and affected parties have identified as being appropriate to measure progress in achieving policy goals. Just as evaluations do not analyze every question that could be asked about the policy and its implementation, not all types of information should be monitored and evaluated. The selection of appropriate indicators is a critical step in planning and conducting evaluations.

For donors or their partners, what is important to track often depends on what their respective governments, the general public, or affected parties expect will be achieved. For donors, accountability often focuses on whether development-assistance resources are used effectively, which may involve monitoring of indicators that describe inputs and outputs to determine how the resources were employed. For donor partners, accountability requires tracking of both process indicators and results indicators because of their need to demonstrate progress as well as the impact of policy reforms. For a given evaluation question, different audiences may expect the question to be answered in different ways. For example, if a policy is designed to reduce nutrient loading, farmer groups will want to know what impact the policy has on net farm incomes, while the public's interest in the policy's impact may well concern water quality. Thus, multiple indicators may be needed to answer a single evaluation question.

Policy implementation will often occur in many steps, taken by numerous ministries and affected parties, and involving a variety of activities. While it is possible to develop indicators to track all of these activities, it may be useful to construct composite indicators or indices to provide a sense of overall progress in implementing the reform. Indicators may not be sufficient to measure impacts and additional analysis may be required. For example, air quality can be monitored but this alone will not permit policy makers to place a value on the benefits of improved quality in terms of health effects. While designing monitoring plans, the acceptance of results indicators as surrogates for impact measures should be discussed and, if not acceptable, plans should be made to conduct supplemental analysis.

Sometimes policy reforms result in different types of successes than were originally envisioned, either for the target reform or for an affected group. For example, a donor-led dialogue related to a specific policy reform may lead assistance partners to adopt and make wider use of participatory processes. A policy may be soundly designed and implemented yet still fail to yield desired results due to exogenous shocks or policy decisions unrelated to the reform. It may be necessary then to document, *ex ante*, the potential of these factors to undermine the policy. Some of these external factors such as inflation, the strength of capital markets, or trends in weather can be monitored along with indicators more directly related to the policy reform.

Assess new policy outcomes to judge success or failure

Evaluation must tell a story—it should provide feedback to policy makers and program managers that can guide diagnosis and changes in policy design and its implementation. Evaluation will be more useful if care is taken to present the problem statement, establish the baseline for comparing the "with and without" (not the "before" and "after") policy scenarios, identify criteria and indicators to monitor change, identify information gaps, plan how to collect data for the analysis, and establish the monitoring schedule to answer the various questions that comprise the evaluation.

Donors and their partners often are reluctant to undertake evaluations of policy reforms because it is difficult to determine unambiguously if the policy is working and to measure its impact. The potential benefits of evaluation as a strategic stage of the policy process are not always appreciated by donors or their partners. Evaluation is not simply a document to satisfy a donor's reporting requirements. A proper evaluation can foster accountability and transparency while providing continuous information on the implementation of the policy. Policy reform can be evaluated if planned in a careful and timely manner, using a well-conceived participatory process.

The role of evaluation is to answer the question: Is the policy working as well as it should? To answer this, an evaluation must assess both the effectiveness of implementation as a process, and the outcome or results of the policy. The implementation effort can be evaluated earlier in the process than results, given the time required for affected parties to respond to the policy change, and for their behavioral responses to result in improvements. External factors may have both positive and negative influences on the performances of policies. It may be necessary to analyze these factors and attribute results to each of the most important factors. For example, periods of recession, high rates of inflation, or unfavorable costs of capital may discourage facilities or other affected parties from undertaking investments in pollution controls, alternative activities, or new methods. The confounding factors in policy success must be factored out of the assessment.

Evaluation is often treated as a discrete one-time analytical exercise rather than a multi-faceted stage of the policy-reform process involving a number of analytical activities. This misperception of evaluation as simply a reporting requirement may account for the lack of interest among donor partners. A single evaluation is of limited use in tracking implementation success, or in analyzing impacts of policy reforms. In addition, if evaluation has not been planned from the beginning of the reform process, the information needed to track progress may be limited, thereby making it difficult to prepare an evaluation report. While the report may be the culmination of this stage of the policy process, evaluation should include many intermediate activities to track and analyze progress. Donors and their partners do not always appreciate the potential benefits of evaluation. For donors, evaluation may be viewed as an obligatory account of assistance resources devoted to projects and programs. Unless donors are explicitly required to analyze the results of the policy reforms, it is less costly in time and funds to limit the focus of their evaluations to the inputs—meetings, funding, agreements—rather than the outputs (new policy outcomes). Very often the beneficial effects of policy reform may occur long after the donor's assistance program is completed. Thus, donors' partners will need to understand the benefits of evaluation in terms of improved accountability and transparency. This will require that evaluations be planned ahead of time, and performance data collected during the assistance program.

A key challenge in evaluation is to "filter out the noise" in order to focus on the relevant information and analyses that answer the question: Is the policy achieving the desired results? The noise occurs because policy reforms are not implemented in a vacuum but are subject to dynamic changes in the political, economic, social, and cultural context. The political and economic setting for implementation is similarly dynamic, with ministries balancing priorities and budgets for a variety of policy reforms. Many voices will often be more convincing than a single voice, and will lend credibility to the policy as well as the policy makers. Evaluation results should be generated at frequent intervals and a dissemination strategy developed to ensure the results are shared widely among implementing ministries, the general public, and affected parties.

The role of external participants

For nearly half a century, a number of industrialized countries have provided technical and financial assistance to the less developed and developing countries around the world. Much of this assistance has been for bricks-and-mortar projects and, more recently, humanitarian relief in response to natural disasters, pandemics, and civil conflict. Donors have also contributed to policy-reform efforts, although since the 1960s, this assistance could not be construed as demand-driven either by recipients or donors. Rather, financial and project assistance was conditioned on the willingness of recipient countries to accept a set of structural adjustment policies that were deemed by donors to be essential in helping recipient countries attain growth in GDP. At the peak, this supply-driven policy assistance, spearheaded by the IMF, the World Bank, and bilateral donors, included as many as 45 policy conditionalities. The logic of these *structural adjustment programs* was very simple— donors thought they would work, based on their success at home, and the insistence on these conditions would be helpful in gaining approval of continued donor funding among national legislatures, the taxpaying public, and member countries of the multilateral banks and financial organization.

While there are good examples—and some supporting evidence—to show that many recipient countries successfully implemented the suite of policy instruments included in structural adjustment programs, there are also many examples suggesting that such policies were resisted, given lip service, promulgated as presidential decrees and special laws, or never actually formalized in laws and regulations. Most studies of foreign aid and structural adjustment programs have reached the same conclusion—locally designed policies and locally led policy reforms are more likely to succeed than those that are tied to donor-assistance packages (Bräutigam and Knack 2004).

Nevertheless, the policy-reform process can benefit from the participation of donors (including international NGOs) as facilitators, technical assistance providers, and partners in advancing reforms. We close this chapter by drawing attention to two important issues: (1) donor participation from the perspective of the nation-state and of the donor; and (2) a brief overview of a set of best practices focused on making policy-reform partnerships work better than is the historic norm. These best practices have been gleaned from the review of more than 75 case studies over the last decade (USAID 2004).

Policy partnerships

Donors and their development partners have always cooperated on a range of foreign aid activities. However, partnering on policy reform is more controversial than collaborating on projects or humanitarian assistance, and *policy partnerships* can bring many special issues into play. As we have stressed previously, successful partnership must find common ground, and they require a shared motivation and commitment. Below, we explore these partnership issues first from the perspective of the nation-state, and then from the perspective of the donor.

The nation-state's perspective on partnering with donors

While developing countries are usually quite receptive to many forms of foreign assistance, they tend to be less open to assistance in the policy-reform process than in programs entailing the transfer of financial resources and projects. After all, policymaking is a core management function of governments and donor assistance in this realm may be perceived as too intrusive and indicate weakness or lack of leadership on the part of the government. The legacy of the structural adjustment programs seems likely to lead the public to conclude that a partnership with a donor promotes the donor's agenda rather than the goals of the country.

These concerns, while understandable, can be overcome if national leaders believe that active donor participation is beneficial to the policy-reform process. In fact, policy partnerships may be coveted by some leaders in order to mobilize the financial means for training, capacity building, education and awareness programs, and to benefit from international policy experience in diagnosis and policy design. Donor assistance may be particularly important to newly-formed governments and those governments recovering from civil strife, natural disasters, or severe

---

ILLUSTRATIVE CASE: ENGAGING HIGH-LEVEL FORUMS TO CHAMPION POLICY CHANGE

In 1994, Egyptian President Hosni Mubarak and U.S. Vice-President Al Gore announced a new initiative, the U.S.–Egyptian Partnership for Economic Growth and Development , designed to consolidate and build on past and present collaboration between the two nations. The partnership also had as one of it goals to propose a new paradigm for growth and development.

One of the four sub-committees for the partnership focused on sustainable development and the environment and was co-chaired by the Egyptian Minister of Environment and USAID Administrator.

With this sub-committee providing senior leadership, high-level visibility and an endorsement that was respected by all parties, Egypt was able to make progress in mitigating lead pollution and adopt a series of policy measures focused on managing the expanding tourism on the Red Sea Coast.

---

economic crises. If viewed as independent parties or honest brokers, donors may be able to help resolve conflicts or mediate an impasse among decision makers and various interest groups when the reform process gets stuck. Donor participation and support for reforms may also help new governments to legitimize and increase their credibility with various interest groups in the process of crafting policy reforms.

National leaders can take steps to establish certain partnerships so as to gain obvious benefits from donor assistance, and to quell concerns that donor participation undermines national sovereignty over the process of institutional change. First, if policy reform accords with current procedures, and if it is conducted in an open, transparent way—and if it welcomes the participation of a wide range of local and national interests—it will be easier to demonstrate that donor participation is strategic and adds real value rather than comprising some unwelcome form of negotiated or imposed reform. It is indeed true that some organizations—and the IMF comes immediately to mind—often negotiate structural adjustments directly with heads of governments rather than advocate such policies within the framework of a broad-based political processes.

Second, many governments can form partnerships with those donors with whom they have long-standing relationships of constructive technical and financial assistance. In such instances, there will be a background of mutual understanding of the policy-reform process within a particular national setting. When this is the case, international partners will enjoy greater credibility with the public and various interest groups than will be the case for donors who are new to the reform process. Donors of long standing are more likely to assist in implementing and evaluating reforms rather than simply promoting a specific set of favored reforms.

Third, there are often very good reasons for a nation-state to enter into partnerships with multiple donors, particularly when the various donors are able to provide different types of support for the reform process. In addition to the obvious synergies that such models provide, a partnership among several donors can help to reduce concerns that individual donors are aggressively advocating specific reforms.

For their part, donors can help to legitimize and add credibility to policy-reform partnerships in terms of how they approach their participation. Does the donor have a specific policy agenda, or does it predicate its participation on the agreement of the government to a pre-determined set of policy options? On the other hand, perhaps the donor is prepared (and perceived) to be an honest broker in the policy-reform process, and is ready to function as a full partner, being both respectful of host-country goals and objectives, and mindful of the sovereignty of the country in the policy-making process.

The donor's perspective on partnering with nation-states

Just as national leaders must consider the advantages and disadvantages of partnerships with donors, the decision to partner with specific nation-states involves similar considerations on the part of donors. Many development projects—roads, water supplies, schools—can yield tangible, quite visible, and immediate benefits. Donors can more readily translate project results into political credibility at home (if a bilateral organization), or in their member countries (if a multilateral organization). On the other hand, when compared to specific projects, policy reform—the crafting of new institutional arrangements—is far slower, more uncertain, and invariably produces winners and losers. It is often the case that the benefits of policy reform may take some years to be fully perceived by the general population. Further, it is more difficult to apportion credit for policy successes than for tangible projects—especially those that leave obvious assets on the ground (dams, roads, schools).

However, support for institutional change, by altering behaviors of individuals and organizations, can result in sustained outcomes and therefore can yield net benefits that far exceed those of one-time project assistance. This is the case because the benefits of policy reform are far-reaching and long-lived, and because policy assistance costs a fraction of the costs of "bricks and mortar" projects. Furthermore, comprehensive participatory policy-reform processes reinforce and promote good governance—an overarching goal of most donor assistance.

As with host-country decision makers, many bi-lateral donors must be accountable to their legislators—and ultimately to their fellow citizens for their activities in developing countries. Donors establish assistance strategies, and international NGOs develop programs and strategic plans, to determine where and how they will work. In some cases, the conditions of engagement may require that host countries adopt a set of policies to access loans, cash transfers, or other forms of financial support. Even if particular nation-states consent to these conditionalities, policy support may still yield uncertain results. The reform process may experience delays, and it may yield outcomes that significantly lag behind a donor's investment in the reform process.

Some of these concerns can be managed by donors. By conducting an assessment of the reform process, and by understanding which reforms are likely to be most contentious, donors can engage the process with appropriately calibrated expectations of the schedule and the requisite financial obligation. One of the most difficult challenges for donors is to demonstrate intermediate results and progress in their support of institutional reform. In legislatures that devote most of their time to domestic economic issues, development agencies are often hard pressed to articulate the benefits of foreign assistance—but particularly in those cases featuring new policies rather than tangible project results. Pressure for enhanced accountability creates problems for policy reforms vis-à-vis more traditional programs and projects.

Best practices for policy-reform partnerships

Once donors and national leaders agree to cooperate in promoting policy reforms, a number of best practices will help donors to be more effective partners.

Understand how the policy reform process is organized and the potential scope for donor participation

Before entering the policy-reform process, donors should invest time to understand how problems are to be diagnosed and new policies designed, assessed, adopted, and implemented. Who are the players? Who is mandated to: (1) lead the process; (2) conduct analysis; (3) present policy options to decision makers; and (4) select new policies? What accommodation for public (and donor) participation is provided? Such analysis will help donors to determine what their potential role might be, and will be essential for them to understand structural or procedural aspects that may influence how long it might take for the reform process to reach fruition.

Assess progress if the process is already underway

In many instances, donors do not join the process at the beginning of problem diagnosis, but arrive much later after several steps have been completed. For example, donors might join the reform process during policy design when the process is stuck and consensus on the choice of policies has been difficult to reach. Or, they may join when there is an obvious need to support implementation activities such as training of agency staff, or to facilitate preparation and dissemination of education and awareness materials. In such cases, donors must take stock of the analysis and decisions that have been taken in earlier stages. One common challenge for donors is when they are brought in to support policy implementation, only to find that there are a large number of serious problems with the new policy. In such cases, donors may need to condition their participation on an agreement with national leaders to review the new policy before continuing with implementation.

Assess and strengthen local capacity to enhance quality and timeliness of the reform process

Just as local-led policy reform will likely be more successful than donor-led reforms, local research institutes and NGOs may be more credible in conducting analyses in support of policy reforms than will foreign experts. Donors should identify and seek to strengthen local organizations to enable them to participate more effectively in the process of institutional change. In addition to their credibility, local organizations will have a better understanding of local political, economic, social, and cultural contexts, they will have better access to information, and they will benefit from a strong relative capacity for working with local interests.

Be flexible in terms of the type of support provided to the process

The policy-reform process is dynamic and subject to a number of changes such as changes in government or leadership of the reform process, unexpected shocks such as civil strife, economic crisis, or natural disasters. Or, the process may simply grind to a halt because certain issues can't be resolved. Donors should be prepared to respond to new requests for support or adjust activities when the process moves in alternative directions. Donors may be asked to bring in outside views or to launch pilot projects of certain policy options, to mediate disagreements among special interests, or to organize study tours to demonstrate successful policies, practices, or technologies in other countries.

Make a commitment to the reform process that is commensurate with resource and temporal dimensions

One of the key problems in partnerships for policy reform is the timeframe of donor projects, through which donors typically provide assessment and capacity-building support. While a three-year donor project may be adequate to support the early stages of problem diagnosis and policy design, later stages will often be critical to the success of the most essential reforms. This follows from the fact that adaptive management to fine-tune policies, or necessary steps to implement certain elements, cannot occur until later in the reform process. Donors typically establish monitoring and evaluation activities focused on projects rather than to gauge progress on the more subtle outcomes of institutional change. As noted earlier, donors face pressure to show results and this makes it difficult to stay engaged over a period that is long enough to observe new policy outcomes. In such cases, where donors cannot extend their participation, they may be able to devote financial resources to assist implementing agencies and/or other participants to build the necessary capacity to monitor and evaluate the implementation of new policies.

Coordinate with other donors

The policy-reform process will often involve two or more donor partners. This can be beneficial to national leaders in demonstrating broad international support for planned reforms. However, it is important to recognize that different donors may come to the task of institutional change with rather different expectations and reform priorities. This implies that the individual contributions of donors will need to be carefully coordinated to avoid duplication of effort or, worse, conflict.

Given the crucial role of national and local leaders in successful problem definition and diagnosis, it is essential that donors respect this fact and mediate their differences in a way that does not jeopardize the fragile relationships between counterparts and those in the donor community. It is acknowledged that the particular imperatives and agendas of different donor agencies can make such an approach difficult. For instance, a particular donor's willingness to fund new policy reforms may be tied to the adoption of specific reforms—in which case this can serve to limit openness and undermine national leadership. Or, because donors may have different visions of the appropriate policy direction, they may exert competing pressures on host-country policy makers. This must be avoided if the diagnostic and design stages are to proceed in a fruitful manner.

Implications

The emphasis here concerns the critical steps from problem diagnosis to the crafting of plausible solutions to those problems. The most important aspect of any development undertaking is to be absolutely clear about the problem requiring attention, and the instrumental policy innovations that seem plausible solutions to that problem. Development assistance must remain humble and modest. We must be cautious in our expectations. Confidence in the quality of analysis is expected. But overconfidence in the results of projects and programs is dangerous. It is important to remember the golden rule of economic policy—*one policy instrument for each problem to be addressed*. We cannot expect a single policy instrument to achieve two or three policy goals. As the old saying has it, "He who chases two rabbits catches neither."

It is practically impossible for developing countries to undertake necessary and meaningful institutional change without the assistance of the international donor community. This does not mean that donors are needed to drive the process forward. It simply means that the donor community can bring essential analytical credibility and political neutrality to a process that is fraught with contention under the best of circumstances. One essential fact of poor countries is that there is precious little economic slack to ease the perceived adjustment costs of economic reforms. It is not easily explained to those close to the margin that short-run costs will pay agreeable dividends over the long run. Every activity, every firm, and every household is already at the margin of economic solvency. The status quo and the acquired gains associated with that circumstance are assiduously defended. We know from prospect theory that individuals are more alert in defending themselves against probable losses than they are in seeking equally "valuable" gains (Kahneman and Tversky 1979).

This reminds us that one essential role for international donors can be to ameliorate the short-run adjustment costs of needed institutional reforms. Obviously this brings to mind the problematic history of structural adjustment programs. But the difference here is profound. We are not discussing the imposed and politically dangerous reforms of the 1980s. The policy-reform process under discussion here is collaborative, mutually formulated, and jointly implemented. The donor community is here conceived of as a partner, not a parent.

9

TOWARD ECONOMIC COHERENCE

A practical guide

> All the objects of human reason or inquiry may naturally be divided into two kinds... Relations of Ideas, and Matters of Fact.[1]
>
> (Hume 1748: 329)

Vulnerability and coherence: the essential nexus

1   Vulnerable people are the cause and the effect of vulnerable states, and therefore vulnerable states are the cause and the effect of vulnerable people;
2   The singular explanation (cause) of vulnerable people and vulnerable states is the persistent inability of national governments to create the conditions for economic coherence;
3   Economic coherence is the end product—the result—of economy-wide institutional arrangements (policies) that establish a constellation of purposeful behavioral incentives at the individual level;
4   Purposeful behavioral incentives reward diligence and forward-looking action;
5   Perverse behavioral incentives defeat individual initiative and instill resignation.

★★★

The new opportunity

Our purpose here has been to explain the fundamental role of institutions (policies) in creating economic coherence. And, when economic coherence is found to be defective, we have offered detailed guidance concerning the process of policy reform—institutional change. It should now be clear that the purpose of policy reform is to solve specific institutional problems—failed irrigation systems, "highway robbery," the resource curse, deficient agricultural extension services, the absence of a tax bargain, defective physical infrastructure—to name only a few. When these institutional problems persist they increase individual and household vulnerability. Nation-states that fail to rectify the problems of vulnerable people cannot avoid becoming vulnerable states.

In the two preceding chapters (Chapters 7 and 8) we offered quite specific detail about how to go about identifying a specific institutional problem, how to diagnose the reasons for that specific problem, how to work with local interests to design new institutions (new policies) to fix that problem, how to implement those new policies, how to collaborate with local interests (and other donors) to facilitate policy reform, and then how to monitor and evaluate whether or not the new policies (new institutions) have indeed fixed the problem.

Our treatment has *not* addressed the common occurrence of donors seeking to solve many problems at the same time. That is, when development-assistance agencies such as the World Bank engage a country in a "poverty reduction strategy" they do not focus on just one or two problems. Rather, they assess a wide range of issues and develop a strategic approach that allows them to work across a broad spectrum of the economy. They do so under the imprimatur of a poverty reduction strategy paper (PRSP). The standard PRSP is a veritable catalogue of problems found in developing countries—frequent interruptions of electricity, bad roads, broken bridges, lack of credit, failing schools, poor sanitation, gender discrimination, government dysfunction, poor public health, deforestation, low agricultural productivity, etc.

Each problem is carefully documented, and the reader is assured that fixing each one is an essential ingredient in "fighting poverty." Various programs and projects will be described as underway, and others will be touted as new initiatives that will most certainly offer good value in the urgent and necessary war on poverty. Missing in such catalogues is any sense of priority for a certain subset of all possible activities. Equally absent is any clear analytical attention to the causal structure that assures the reader that indeed investing in, say, drinking water will assuredly defeat poverty. Much is taken on faith. There is "analytical faith" resting on the premise that this is now well understood in the literature and does not to be shown here again. And then there is "pure faith" suggesting that fighting poverty is a moral obligation and therefore most anything that is done under that mantle will, most certainly, do good. It may be impossible to prove this, but in this realm of development assistance, proof is superfluous. It is necessary here to point out that too much of what is done in the realm of development assistance rests on faith.

There is now, it would seem, an escape from faith. The activity known as *growth diagnostics* seeks to introduce analytical rigor into economic reform (Hausmann, Rodrik, and Velasco 2006). Decision trees will be constructed to trace out where one might find the most serious binding constraint to growth. A complete analysis of such growth diagnostics will reveal, in lexical progression, the high-payoff investments and policy reforms that will maximize welfare in each country. In its full manifestation, social welfare is maximized by working our way along the chain of binding constraints until the benefits of the last reform are brought into line with the costs of achieving that reform.

While growth diagnostics is a commendable improvement over faith, the approach suffers two serious flaws. First, it brings a misleading appearance of rigor to the job. Second, it starts at the wrong place and then stops short of what is necessary to bring clarity to the development challenge.

Concerning the appearance of rigor, we quote from the creators of growth diagnostics:

> In a low-income country, economic activity must be constrained by at least one of the following two factors: either the cost of finance is too high, or the private return to investment is too low. If the problem is with low private returns, that in turn must be due either to low economic (social) returns or to a large gap between social and private returns (what we refer to as low private appropriability). The first step in the diagnostic analysis is to figure out which of these conditions more accurately characterizes the economy in question.
>
> (Hausmann, Rodrik, and Velasco 2006: 3–4)

Notice the appeal here to well-calibrated macroeconomic models that can not only identify private and social rates of return, but can also reveal where, exactly, in a thoroughly clunky economy, the real culprit is to be found. Can it really be that economic activity in such countries must be constrained by "at least one of the following two factors"—either the cost of finance is too high, or the private return to investment is too low.[2] Is this all there is? Are these really the only two causes of persistent dysfunction? And then of course, we see that low private returns are due to just two more things—low "social" returns or to a large gap between social and private returns. Are these the only possibilities? Do these simple rates of return exhaust the set of plausible reasons for vulnerable people and vulnerable states?

Aside from the serious flaw of contrived completeness, we must recall that the necessary data to conjure models such as this are rarely available, and even less reliable. More seriously, by the time the data are available and rendered into a diagnostic model, what provenance remains? We necessarily conclude that an approach of this sort, perhaps appropriate for what the International Monetary Fund seeks to do, is quite inappropriate for designing development-assistance programs aimed at addressing the manifold problems of vulnerable people stuck in vulnerable states. Moreover, while this exercise in welfare economics may be suited for teaching graduate students, we very much dispute the notion that its practicality extends beyond the classroom. In fact, we are reminded of a famous aphorism by the German philosopher Georg C. Lichtenberg to the effect that: "Delight at having understood a very abstract and obscure system leads most people to believe in the truth of what it demonstrates" (Lichtenberg 1789).

The second flaw of growth diagnostics is that its implied quest for reasons starts in the wrong place, and thus carries the great risk of stopping short of what is required if one is to acquire a comprehensive assessment of the causes of economic dysfunction. Recall our quote above from one of the intellectual fathers of development economics—Joseph Schumpeter—that any effort to explain economic phenomena by reference only to economic phenomena introduces a fatal circularity into economic work. Growth diagnostics suffers this defect. That is, the approach advocated by Hausmann, Rodrik, and Velasco starts its admirable curiosity with reference to rates of return. Starting here means that it will be all too easy to suspend curiosity as soon as some other "economic" reason emerges as the proximate cause of these low returns. Soon, the economic diagnosis becomes caught in its own cycle and therefore misses the real underlying reasons for sweeping dysfunction.

Following Schumpeter, the earnest diagnostician would not stop but would then ask why, exactly, are rates of return so low. Is it because of "highway robbery"? Is it because air pollution destroys market-grade vegetables? Is it because highways are horrible and bridges are in disrepair? Why, exactly, are rates of return so low? As our discussion of abduction makes clear, the real reason—the explanation—must lie beyond economic indicators. Recall that market signals emanate from a confluence of the *Data* and the *Institutional Context* (Figure 2.1). Proper diagnosis must move beyond the façade—the mask—of economic signals if we are to understand vulnerable people and vulnerable states. As we saw with abduction, diagnostic explorations must go beyond economic data—which are mere artifacts of other underlying physical facts and phenomena in the economy.

Creating economic coherence requires a very different approach from that offered through growth diagnostics. Economic coherence can only come from a diagnostic approach that seeks an understanding of the most pressing (binding) *physical constraints* in an economy. Only when those physical constraints are comprehended—and explained—is it possible to turn attention to the design of development strategies that will address the problems of vulnerable people and vulnerable states. Those development policies must address both physical constraints in the economy as well as institutional constraints.

Vulnerable states

At the beginning of the twenty-first century it would certainly be plausible to consider Iraq a vulnerable state. In 2010, the United Nations produced *The Iraq Briefing Book* spelling out the many problems, constraints, and pressing challenges facing the people of Iraq (UNDP 2010).[3] To gain insights into the real challenge of meaningful diagnostics, we will draw upon that report to illustrate our approach to policy diagnostics. We note that the document is 125 single-spaced pages covering every possible aspect of the Iraqi economy—statements of existing binding constraints, key issues, and recommendations for development assistance. For our purposes, we will focus on but four to five single-spaced pages of that full report, reproducing here the discussion of but three sectors in the economy: (1) water, sanitation, and municipal services; (2) transport; and (3) electricity generation and distribution. Our purpose in doing so is to remind the reader that when donors first engage a country for the purpose of bringing about economic change, this is what that engagement looks like. Notice that it is not an engagement rich with elaborate macroeconomic models. Rather, the engagement gets underway with a daunting immersion into a litany of pressing problems.

To quote from the UN *Iraq Briefing Book*:

WATER, SANITATION AND MUNICIPAL SERVICES

Years of conflict, misdirected resources and the effects of centralized command have stifled Iraq's economic growth and development and curtailed investment in new infrastructure and maintenance of existing civic infrastructure. This problem has been particularly acute in the water supply, sanitation and irrigation services sub-sectors due to a lack of preventive maintenance (since the 1980s) and heavy dependence on public budgetary support. The effectiveness of service organizations to meet daily requirements for water (for drinking and for irrigation) has greatly diminished. As a result, most Iraqis now have limited access to a clean water supply, or to sanitation and refuse collection. Serious environmental and health risks associated with contaminated water supplies and inappropriate handling of solid waste and sewage disposal threaten to add to the burden of the already overstretched health system. The concentration of economic and social activities in the main urban centres of Iraq has also led to a proliferation of under-serviced neighbourhoods in major Iraqi cities.

Key Issues

While oil-generated resources may be the key to Iraq's future, clean water is a far more pressing concern: An immediate intervention to provide safe drinking water, adequate sewage collection and treatment services is critical to safeguard public health, raise living standards and protect the environment. Shortages of water supply and sanitation services are acutely felt in urban centers where the majority of Iraqis now live. Outside of Baghdad, potable water service coverage averages below 70 per cent and as low as 48 per cent in rural areas. In Baghdad, as many as 25 per cent of residents remain disconnected from the water supply network and rely on expensive alternative sources of drinking water.

Wastewater collection and treatment rates are even lower than those of potable water: For example, 28.4 per cent of the population in 2000 had access to a sewer system with treatment facilities, a figure that dropped to 9 per cent in 2007. With sewage treatment capacities dropping between 10 and 50 per cent of that which was planned, it is estimated that 50 per cent of wastewater collected is discharged into rivers without any treatment. Of particular concern is existing treatment facilities in Baghdad which are nearly non-operational. It is estimated that 75 per cent of wastewater is channelled untreated into the Tigris river. In addition, water treatment plants in Basrah (12 in number) have a total capacity of approximately 412,000 tons a day which falls significantly short of meeting the maximum demand of about 914,000 tons a day. As a result, some 70 per cent of households in Basrah have access to water supply services for less than 12 hours a day, while the quality of treated water is less than satisfactory.

The situation in KRG is similar in that the facilities have aged, which has markedly decreased the region's ability to draw and purify water. With no option other than to impose restrictions, water is supplied approximately one hour a day in Sulaimaniya and Dohuk governorates, and four to five hours a day in Erbil governorate which is far short of the amount required. In Erbil, the capacity of the three water treatment plants is approximately 241,000 cubic metres (m3) a day, considerably short of the daily demand of 442,000 m3. In Halabja, in Sulaimaniya governorate, there are no water treatment plants, and residents must rely on springs and ground water as water sources. The capacity of the water supply is approximately 18,000 m3 a day, well short of the daily demand of 57,000 m3. Additionally, in Kurdistan, much of the water piping was laid before 1950s and it has significantly deteriorated.

(UN *Iraq Briefing Book* 2010: 91–2)

TRANSPORT

Once regarded as having one of the Middle East's most comprehensive transportation systems, Iraq has suffered from more than two decades of neglect and under-investment in all modes of transport, including road, rail, air and maritime. Between 1980 and 2003, regional conflict, the utilization of public resources to support military initiatives, an extended period of economic sanctions, and deferred maintenance all contributed towards a general decline in the quality of transport facilities and services, and to huge losses in rolling stock. With the onset of the 2003 military intervention, many assets were damaged due to the heavy bombing that occurred, while the looting that followed stripped ministries and transport facilities of equipment, machinery, furniture and supplies. In addition to these challenges, Iraq must transition from a centrally planned command economy to one that is market-based. As a result, the country still faces enormous challenges in reconstructing its transportation networks, facilities, strategic planning and institutional capacities, as well as in re-establishing key transport services.

Key Issues

Loss of key road and bridge assets: In a large country such as Iraq, roads play a central role in the movement of people and goods. A large portion of Iraq's 42,000-kilometre road network is however, in immediate need of rehabilitation. Most of the road network was developed in the 1970s and 1980s, and little new construction has taken place since. Backlogs of maintenance have accumulated over the years, and pavements have failed in many areas. Village access roads have been neglected to the extent that reconstruction rather than rehabilitation is needed along much of the rural road network. The deterioration of village roads has diminished access to markets and social services in many rural areas. In addition, as a result of the first Gulf war and subsequent conflicts, many bridges were damaged, with some key bridges never replaced. Instead, temporary structures (floating bridges) were put in place.

Weakened or lost capacity for quality control and management of the road network: Government road laboratories were decimated by looting in 2003. Not only were equipment and supplies stolen, but institutional capacity of both central and regional facilities was also negatively impacted. These laboratories played an important role in controlling the quality of road construction. Capacity for road network management has historically been strong and adequate in Iraq. Reliance on outdated procedures and equipment has unfortunately, eroded skills and abilities.

Iraq's extensive railway network suffers from poor condition of tracks and equipment: Derailments on the network operated by the Iraqi Railways Corporation are frequent despite speed restrictions. Telecommunications and signalling systems are not functional, and train movements are presently controlled using *ad hoc* methods that do not ensure safety while hampering the capacity of lines. In addition, productivity at the Railways Corporation, which has complete control of the sector, is low and staff members, while technically skilled, have limited exposure to modern managerial techniques and lack the discipline of commercially run organizations.

The country's seaports also suffer from insufficient and obsolete equipment: Proper maintenance has not been undertaken for many years. All Iraqi ports (Umm Qasr, Khor al-Zubair, Basrah, Abu Flus, Abu al-Khasib and Faw) are situated along or inland from the short stretch of coastline between the borders of Iran and Kuwait. Presently, the ports of Umm Qasr and Khor al-Zubair handle about 25 per cent of total imports into Iraq, but they have the potential to become major cargo and container handling facilities. In particular, Umm Qasr, which has a rated capacity of 10 million tons a year and good intermodal road and rail connections, is a vital node for international trade. While its infrastructure is generally in good condition, the port's waterway, superstructure and equipment are not. Significant port assets are in an abandoned state. Chronic siltation and wrecked vessels in approach channels pose additional challenges to increasing traffic volume. In the past, Basrah was the main port in Iraq, but now, like Abu Flus and Abu al-Khasib, it is unusable because of the many sunken vessels that block its waterway access.

The looting after the 2003 conflict devastated bus fleets, public transport offices, and maintenance facilities: These events have exerted tremendous pressure on public transport systems and services which are the only means of affordable transport to the majority of Iraqis. Ensuring mobility and affordable access to jobs, education and health services remains a key issue, especially in the fast growing metropolitan area of Baghdad. A tremendous increase in the number of aged private cars exacerbates congestion and air pollution, and makes mobility and access to job opportunities difficult, especially for the poor.

(UN *Iraq Briefing Book* 2010: 117–18)

ELECTRICITY

Electricity demand has increased significantly and by approximately 6 per cent a year over the last three years. Electricity supply in 2009 was at about 67 per cent of peak demand, with periods of blackout still averaging nationally more than 9 hours a day. The current supply situation is exacerbated by deteriorated network conditions brought on by many years without appropriate new investment, which has left all three components of the system – generation, transmission, and distribution – in a significantly degraded condition. Electricity shortages have been mitigated only somewhat by a 119 per cent increase in the import of electricity from neighbouring countries from March 2008 to March 2010. Inadequate electricity is seen by Iraqis today as a top concern, impacting on their daily life and family, compared to other matters such as national security, health care, unemployment, crime, high prices, etc. Moreover, inadequate and poor electricity services and infrastructure impede private sector development and negatively affect employment and economic growth. These shortages are creating hardship and undermining government credibility. In addition to the continuing need for investments in transmission and distribution, adding new power generation capacity is of crucial importance. Electricity supply remained almost stagnant from mid-2004 to mid-2007 at approximately 90,000 MWH of daily supply. Starting in September 2007, a major push to expand generation and improve the transmission system led to significant gains in electricity supply, hitting a high of 169,000 MWH (just over 7,000MW of generation capacity) in March 2010. Improving electricity supply is a significant priority for the government. The Ministry of Electricity (MoEI) is currently working on ambitious plans to develop 15,000MW of new generation capacity by the end of 2014, and plans a significant increase in crude oil production and refining which will yield additional heavy fuel oil, refined products, and natural gas to fuel these power stations. In addition priority rehabilitation projects are planned for existing assets, and the strengthening of transmission and distribution networks to accommodate additional supply. Access to sufficient capital to finance this generation expansion has proven difficult, and the MOEI has also embarked upon an ambitious programme to attract private investment through Independent Power Producer

(IPP) projects for almost 4,000MW of new power stations. However, these plans have been under preparation for a long time and are not yet completed nor developed into a project-specific implementation strategy for the electricity. Hydroelectric production declined from 30.8 per cent of the total of electricity produced in Iraq in 1996 to 17.5 per cent in 2006. In the long term, and considering the time frame for appropriate investment, there is good potential for hydro and for other renewable sources of energy – particularly solar sector.

(UN *Iraq Briefing Book* 2010: 111–12)

The first thing to notice about the language in *The Iraq Briefing Book* is that it not only covers what is said to be wrong with the Iraqi economy—the facts and phenomena—but it also ranges far and wide concerning ad hoc diagnoses ("X happens because of Y"), and it is clear about what should be done immediately—it offers quite explicit policy prescriptions. A quick survey of the above few pages reveals approximately 52 statements concerning facts and phenomena ("P is Q"). We can think of these as assessments of the situation on the ground. There are over 30 diagnostic assertions ("Q is R") meaning that the authors of the report are sure that "R causes Q." And then there are nine policy prescriptions ("S is ~R") indicating what should be done (S) to rectify a particular problem (R). In other words we find here, in approximately 4 percent of *The Iraq Briefing Book*, almost 100 assertions concerning facts and phenomena, the causes of (the explanation for) the facts and phenomena, and prescriptions about what urgent actions ought to be taken.

This jumble of diagnostic claims and policy prescriptions conveys an aura of policy certitude that is highly problematic. How do the authors know, and here we mean *really* know, with such confidence, that Q is R? And how can they be sure that S is ~R? It is important to keep in mind that every policy prescription (S) is, at the same time, a prediction (~R). The authors of the report, and we see this in the standard poverty reduction strategy papers, are really quite sure that doing S will indeed solve the causal factor R, and thereby correct the problem Q. But how can they be so sure of their diagnosis—and therefore their policy prescription? What evidence have they adduced to make the case that their diagnosis is correct? Without careful analysis, how can they be so sure about the predictions embedded in their prescriptions?

In sum, it is impossible to read this relatively minor portion (4 percent) of the large *Iraq Briefing Book* without a feeling of despair. With over 100 assertions of facts and phenomena, of diagnosis, and of policy prescriptions contained in but a fraction of the report, the mind grows numb at the enormity of the task ahead. What will be found in the remaining 120 pages? While it is fair to conclude that one becomes informed by consulting so many facts and phenomena, by pondering the extensive diagnostic assertions, and by considering the development prescriptions, a more honest reaction is that of incapacity—paralysis. Where should serious work start? How to decide what is the most binding constraint? How is it possible to undertake growth diagnostics—with its focus on public and private rates of return—in the face of this super-abundance of claims and assertions? Which, out of hundreds, are the most important binding constraints to growth?

Obviously, this last is the wrong question. In an economy with several hundred serious problems, the very idea that there is a single most important binding constraint is meaningless.[4] It is not even possible to conjure a list of the five most important binding constraints to growth. Is electricity more important than water?[5] Is water more important than oil? Is oil more important than transport? Is increasing the hours per day of electricity more important than more reliable water supplies? Who can possibly know?

Luckily, there is an escape from this impossible task of "knowing." The escape is to deploy a process whose purpose is that of fostering mutual learning. As we stressed in Chapter 7, the policy-reform process is really a search for what seems possible to do when there are many things that are impossible to do. Humans do not know what it is they really want until they work their way toward figuring out what they might be able to have (Bromley 2006). That is what restaurant menus are for.

Turning now to a process that avoids the obvious futility of finding the most important binding constraint, it is well to realize that when national leaders and their development-assistance counterparts engage in an honest and respectful policy dialogue, the serious conversation concerns contending empirical claims about the future and how to get there. As we said earlier (Chapter 7), thinking about the future concerns consideration of contending "created imaginings" (Bromley 2006; Shackle 1961). Missing in such conversations is any thought of which policies would be the most efficient to pursue. It is also clear that welfare economics—and benefit–cost analysis—would be unlikely topics of careful deliberation. While rates of return may arise, it would do so in discussions of detailed comparisons between two equally attractive industrial projects. Conversations about schooling, gender empowerment, sanitation, environmental conservation, and child labor would not be burdened with such impertinences.

Now suppose such discussions took place against the background of a document such as *The Iraq Briefing Book*. It would carry the presumption of a plausible place to start. There is certainly an abundance of facts and phenomena already compiled by respected experts from a wide array of international organizations. The groundwork has already been laid. The obvious first step would be to ignore the diagnostic claims and the policy prescriptions. They must be ignored because they are not to be trusted. But the abundant claims about the facts on the ground—"P is Q"—are a plausible place to start. The complete list of such problems must be understood, however, as mere suggestions.

By this we mean that this long list must be treated as ideas worthy of further work. Referring back to Chapter 7, the necessary activity associated with problems is to figure out why those problems—those facts and phenomena—exist. Notice that the answer to why those problems exist constitutes the necessary explanation for their existence. That is the purpose of diagnosis. As we saw in Chapter 6, the route toward explanation runs through abduction:

The surprising fact C is observed.
If A were true then C would be expected (and therefore not surprising).
Since C is indeed observed, A must be true.

And so the earnest development expert must become concerned with the composition of the vector A. Also recall that the most obvious explanations, often called the efficient (or proximate) causes may themselves require yet further explanation.

It is now possible to elaborate the singular importance of careful diagnosis. Most obviously, it is diagnosis that leads to plausible explanations as to why the facts and phenomena exist. Equally important, this understanding of the reasons for the existence of specific problems will then illuminate the way toward what will become specific findings and recommendations—policy prescriptions. But notice that the diagnostic phase, to be useful, must be *recursive rather than linear*. As seen above, the rather standard approach is to compile a catalogue of problematic facts and phenomena about a country and its economy. Many poverty reduction strategy papers (PRSPs) have this flavor. Continuing on this trajectory means that everything that seems troubling about the economy is swept up and included in the general problem assessment. Whether large or small, whether profound or merely interesting, whether documented or anecdotal, all of these problems take on equal importance. This is apparent in *The Iraq Briefing Book*.[6]

The formulation of development programs and projects must be recursive because it is necessary to work iteratively between the catalogue of facts and phenomena that seem to be problems for the economy, and various diagnostic protocols. This recursive approach will be important in determining whether or not it is possible to work out—drawing on economic theory and knowledge of the economy under discussion—plausible and meaningful reasons for what we observe with respect to each of those "problems" (those facts and phenomena). If the reasons for, or the causes of, a particular problem are elusive—we cannot understand it, or we cannot explain why the problem occurs—then we must drop that particular problem for our list of important issues warranting attention. After all, if it is impossible to figure out why a particular problem exists, the development expert will be at a complete loss to offer advice how to rectify it. And if a particular problem cannot plausibly be rectified then it is programmatically irrelevant. Development assistance must economize on the need for analytical work. And development assistance must focus on the important and *correctable* problems.

The essential point here is that development assistance efforts must concentrate limited time and financial resources on a subset of all problems—the *actionable facts and phenomena*—rather than on just any facts and phenomena. As immediately above, exquisite attention must be paid to those issues—those impediments and symptoms of impediments—that seem implicated in the overall economic malaise under discussion. That is the necessary condition for inclusion in a list of pressing development problems. But the sufficient condition for inclusion in the list of issues that will actually be addressed first is that the analyst can also offer insights as to why fixing a special subset of that longer list will be salutary for the well-being of the economy.

The recursive nature of getting a grip on which problems warrant immediate attention means that the development analyst will work back and forth between the long catalogue of facts and phenomena and the analyst's ability to explain those facts and phenomena. This back and forth will allow the analyst to squeeze down (to compact) the scope and reach of problems to be addressed. As the process moves forward, it is essential that the three aspects of analysis be kept separate and distinct—yet linked. That is, there must be a clear demarcation between activities focused on *assessment* ("P is Q"), on *diagnosis* ("Q is R"), and the development of recommendations or *prescriptions* ("S is ~R").

As above, every prescription ("S is ~R") is a prediction that S will correct R and thereby rectify Q. With the predictive content of development prescriptions in mind, it becomes obvious why the subset of actionable facts and phenomena must be derived from the ability to understand and explain their reasons and causes—that is, from good diagnostics. If the analyst can do that, then the ground will be firm for the derivation of prescriptions with plausible predictive power: "Yes we are now sure, doing S will indeed fix R, and if R is corrected, then Q will no longer be a problem." Unfortunately, this degree of certitude is harder than it seems. The analyst does not have the luxury of guesses and abstract claims from economic theory. Evidence must be marshaled.

Getting to work

The creation of this compressed list of actionable problems to be addressed brings us to the difficult task of implementation. We have covered a number of aspects of this daunting challenge in Chapter 7. Here we offer an additional step—a method for judging the urgency and instrumentality of the set of actionable facts and phenomena. Notice that we are offering a more feasible and workable approach to devising program priorities than the quixotic search for the most important binding constraint. Nor are we interested in assessing social and private rates of return.

When considering the many impediments in the economy, the short list of urgent and important problems to be rectified can be worked out by focusing on those problems for which:[7] (1) the shadow price of the constraint is high—a *promising payoff* is available from relaxing the constraint; (2) the target efficiency of relaxing the constraint is high—the constraint is efficaciously *instrumental to a clear goal*; (3) policy entrepreneurs are willing, with the appropriate assistance, to work on behalf of changing the constraint—*latent agency is present*; (4) a few agents in the economy have a history of efforts to change the constraint—there is evidence of *prior commitment*; and (5) there is a general consensus among important political leaders that this is a high-priority battle worth the expenditure of political capital—the *benefits of change outweigh the costs of not changing*.[8]

With this operational template in hand, development planners can begin the process of working through the long litany of problems and economic impediments. It may be noticed, with careful thought, that picking through the long list of problems crying out for remediation with the aid of these five conditions would move the analyst very close to a ranking of the most important binding constraints. We have selection criteria that reward high payoff, target efficiency, effective agency, plausible commitment, and political consensus. What more could one ask for?

Notice that this approach is not dependent on conjured notions of rates of return derived from flawed data. We rely, instead, on careful assessments by knowledgable experts—national leaders, university experts, and members of the international donor community. Recall that even the most "rigorous" of macroeconomic models, including elaborate efforts at social benefit–cost analysis, could produce only the appearance of accuracy. The precision suggested by formal analyses carried out to several decimal points is an example of false consciousness. There is little demand for misleading precision.

Implications

Our commitment to economic coherence is predicated on solid theoretical and empirical evidence that the separate pieces of an economy must fit together in such a way that the agents in that economy—members of households and firms—are led (given incentives and sanctions) to act in ways that benefit them, and in doing so will, thereby, bring about gradual increments to economic growth and improvements in general economic circumstances. We are aware that this is Adam Smith's metaphor of the "invisible hand." We embrace it here without apology.

But, as in more important realms of life, a ready embrace—if not followed up with sincere mutual commitments—is worse than no embrace at all. The abiding proviso that must accompany Smith's celebration of possessive individualism—a caveat that Smith understood well, though it is ignored by fervent market fundamentalists—is that those beneficial market signals do not appear from heaven as if by magic. The conditions for efficacious signaling in a market economy must be created, they must be nurtured, and they must be supported. That is the role of the political community—the state.

The development catechism of the past several decades has invoked magic and faith—magic in the notion that markets work best when governments are weak and irrelevant, and faith in the notion that doing what is laid out in economic textbooks is both necessary and sufficient for economic progress. Magic and faith have not been kind to the world's vulnerable people and vulnerable states.

NOTES

1 From convergence to coherence: the new development opportunity

1 "Global Hunger and Food Security," http://www.state.gov/documents/organization/129768.pdf, accessed 29 February 2012.
2 There is a related literature on "poverty traps" that has gained some attention in the past decade. We do not find the concept to be very useful (Azariadis 1996).

2 On economic coherence

1 We show this in greater detail in Chapter 6.
2 One often sees expression of a need for strong protection of property rights. Unfortunately, this is incomplete. Landless people in Southeast Asia or Latin America hardly benefit from "strengthened" property rights—the very legal condition that keeps them landless.
3 http://web.worldbank.org/WBSITE/EXTERNAL/EXTABOUTUS/0,,pagePK:5000 4410 piPK:36602 theSitePK:29708,00.html, accessed 24 October 2011.

3 Contending with economic incoherence: the notional state

1 This was referred to as the *Data* in Figures 2.1 and 2.2.

4 Creating coherence: the role of institutions

1 When the subject of compulsion and obedience arises, the question quickly turns to compliance and enforcement. Our concern here is with the existence of rules and their effects, assuming that compliance is generally attained.
2 One will sometimes see reference to "de facto rights." Unfortunately, this is a logical impossibility. Because rights are legal relations, granted by authoritative agents (legislatures, courts) they cannot be mere "de facto" in nature. They are *de jure* or they are nothing at all. Perhaps those who use this language mean "presumptive rights"? That is, individuals presume (act as if) they have rights when they do not.

6 The diagnostic imperative

1 Notice the vector notation (underlined) on $\underline{A}$. We do this to remind the reader that the constituents of $\underline{A}$ are indeed several in number—$a_1, a_2, a_3, \ldots, a_n$.

2 Those who insist that prices "come from" markets reveal themselves capable of believing that milk "comes from" bottles.

9 Toward economic coherence: a practical guide

1 This is known as Hume's Fork.

2 Notice the full meaning of the phrase "economic activity must be constrained by at least one of the following two factors." Reworded in the interest of clarity, this phrase is properly rendered as: "There are only two factors that constrain economic activity..."

3 The briefing book was prepared by members of the Iraq Partners Forum. It benefited from inputs and contributions from officials from Canada, Denmark, the European Union, Japan, Italy, Poland, the United Kingdom, the United States, the World Bank, FAO1, ILO, IOM, OHCHR, UNAMI, UNDP, UNESCO, UNFPA, UN-HABITAT, UNHCR, UNICEF, UNIDO, UNIFEM, UNOPS, WFP, WHO, and the OECD.

4 And we wish to stress that the problems in Iraq, though plausibly related to the decade of war and civil strife, are not materially different from the problems encountered in many countries in Africa. Any differences are of degree, not of kind.

5 And we see here a fundamental problem with country assessments that start with a preoccupation for economic growth. If electricity is more important than water for growth, does that necessarily imply that electricity is more important than water for people and their participation in the economy? We suggest that it would be very hard to sustain that argument.

6 This problem is inherent in the very process of compiling such detailed information across so many aspects of a national economy. Experts from each of the "sectors" will be enlisted to prepare assessment reports. The problems will be carefully noted and described (assessments). The reasons for those problems (diagnoses) will be advanced with great certitude—after all, that is what experts are for. And then high-priority actions (policy prescriptions) will be proposed because that is why experts are brought in. When all of these independent and quite disconnected reports are compiled into a single document, the resulting catalogue is incomprehensible concerning which activities, out of several hundred, are really important and urgent. Each expert, of course, is sure of it.

7 These conditions are a variation of those suggested by Hausmann, Rodrik, and Velasco (2006). Despite our misgivings over most aspects of growth diagnostics, the authors offer a valuable screening protocol which we are happy to endorse.

8 Notice the presumption that political leaders have some general sense of "benefits and costs" broadly defined. While some economists will object, most democracies function on this very presumption.

BIBLIOGRAPHY

Arndt, H. W. (1987) *Economic Development: the history of an idea*, Chicago: University of Chicago Press.

Azariadis, C. (1996) "The Economics of Poverty Traps Part One: complete markets", *Journal of Economic Growth*, 1: 449–86.

Baland, J.-M. and J.-P. Platteau (1996) *Halting Degradation of Natural Resources*, Oxford: Clarendon Press.

Balint, P.J. and J. Mashinya (2006) "The Decline of a Model Community-Based Conservation Project: governance, capacity, and devolution in Mahenye, Zimbabwe", *Geoforum*, 37: 805–15.

Barrett, C.B. and P. Arcese (1998) "Wildlife Harvest in Integrated Conservation and Development Projects: linking harvest to household demand, agricultural production and environmental shocks in the Serengeti", *Land Economics*, 74(4): 449–65.

—— and B. Swallow (2006) "Fractal Poverty Traps", *World Development*, 34(1): 1–15.

Becker, L.C. (1977) *Property Rights*, London: Routledge & Kegan Paul.

Bernstein, R. (1983) *Beyond Objectivism and Relativism: science, hermeneutic, and praxis*, Philadelphia: University of Pennsylvania Press.

Bigsten, A. (2002) "Can Africa Catch Up?", *World Economics*, 3(2): 17–33.

Boyes, W. and M. Melvin (2005) *Economics*, Boston: Houghton Mifflin.

Bräutigam, D. and S. Knack (2004) "Foreign Aid, Institutions and Governance in Sub-Saharan Africa", *Economic Development and Cultural Change*, 52: 255–85.

Brock, W.A. and S.N. Durlauf (2001) "Growth Economics and Reality", *World Bank Economic Review*, 15(2): 229–72.

——, S.N. Durlauf, and K.D. West (2003) "Policy Evaluation in Uncertain Environments", *Brookings Papers on Economic Activity*, 1: 235–322.

Bromley, D.W. (1989a) *Economic Interests and Institutions: the conceptual foundations of public policy*, Oxford: Blackwell.

—— (1989b) "Property Relations and Economic Development: the other land reform", *World Development*, 17(6): 867–77.

—— (1991) *Environment and Economy: property rights and public policy*, Oxford: Blackwell.

—— (1995) "Development Reconsidered: the African challenge", *Food Policy*, 20(5): 425–38.

—— (2000) "Property Regimes and Pricing Regimes in Water Resource Management", in A. Dinar (ed.) *The Political Economy of Water Pricing Reforms*, Oxford: Oxford University Press (ch. 2).

—— (2006) *Sufficient Reason: volitional pragmatism and the meaning of economic institutions*, Princeton: Princeton University Press.

—— (2008a) "Resource Degradation in the African Commons: accounting for institutional decay", *Environment and Development Economics*, 13: 539–63.

—— (2008b) "Formalising Property Relations in the Developing World: the wrong prescription for the wrong malady", *Land Use Policy*, 26: 20–7.

—— (2008c) "Volitional Pragmatism", *Ecological Economics*, 68: 1–13.

—— and J.-P. Chavas (1989) "On Risk, Transactions, and Economic Development in the Semiarid Tropics", *Economic Development and Cultural Change*, 37(4): 719–36.

—— and J.D. Foltz (2011) "Sustainability under Siege: transport costs and corruption on West Africa's trade corridors", *Natural Resources Forum*, 35: 32–48.

—— and I.D. Hodge (1990) "Private Property Rights and Presumptive Policy Entitlements: reconsidering the premises of rural policy", *European Review of Agricultural Economics*, 17: 197–214.

—— and Y. Yao (2006) "Understanding China's Economic Transformation: are there lessons here for the developing world?", *World Economics*, 7(2): 73–95.

Brunnschweiler, C. and E.H. Bulte (2008) "The Resource Curse Revisited and Revised: a tale of paradoxes and red herrings", *Journal of Environmental Economics and Management*, 55: 248–64.

Burnside, C. and D. Dollar (2000) "Aid, Policies, and Growth", *American Economic Review*, 90(4): 847–68.

Carter M.R. and C.B. Barrett (2006) "The Economics of Poverty Traps and Persistent Poverty: an asset-based approach", *Journal of Development Studies*, 42(2): 178–99.

Cheung, S.N.S. (1983) "The Contractual Nature of the Firm", *Journal of Law and Economics*, 26: 1–22.

Christman, J. (1994) *The Myth of Property*, Oxford: Oxford University Press.

Clark, C.W. (1973) "Profit Maximization and the Extinction of Animal Species", *Journal of Political Economy*, 81: 950–61.

Collier, P. (2007) *The Bottom Billion*, Oxford: Oxford University Press.

Commons, J.R. (1924) *Legal Foundations of Capitalism*, London: Macmillan.

de Soto, H. (2000) *The Mystery of Capital*, New York: Basic Books.

Easterly, W. (2001) *The Elusive Quest for Growth*, Cambridge: MIT Press.

—— (2006) *The White Man's Burden: why the West's efforts to aid the rest have done so much ill and so little good*, New York: Penguin.

—— (2007) "Was Development Assistance a Mistake?", *American Economic Review*, 97(2): 328–32.

—— and R. Levine (1997) "Africa's Growth Tragedy", *Quarterly Journal of Economics*, 112(4): 1203–50.

Glendon, M.A. (1991) *Rights Talk: the impoverishment of political discourse*, New York: Free Press.

Hausmann, R., D. Rodrik, and A. Velasco (2006) "Getting the Diagnosis Right", *Finance and Development*, 43(1): 1–9.

Herbst, J. (2000) *States and Power in Africa*, Princeton: Princeton University Press.

Hohfeld, W.N. (1917) "Fundamental Legal Conceptions as Applied in Judicial Reasoning", *Yale Law Journal*, 26: 710–70.

Hume, D. (1748) *An Inquiry Concerning Human Understanding*, Section IV, Part I, http://www.davidhume.org/texts/ehv (accessed 1 March 2012).

Jackson, R.H. and C.G. Rosberg (1982) "Why Africa's Weak States Persist: the empirical and the juridical in statehood", *World Politics*, 35(1): 1–24.

Kahneman, D. and A. Tversky (1979) "Prospect Theory: an analysis of decision under risk", *Econometrica*, 47: 263–91.

Kakwani, N. and H.H. Son (2006) *New Global Poverty Counts*, United Nations Development Programme.

Kamarck, A.M. (1976) *The Tropics and Economic Development: a provocative inquiry into the poverty of nations*, Baltimore: Johns Hopkins University Press.

Kronman, A.T. (1985) "Contract Law and the State of Nature", *Journal of Law, Economics, and Organization*, 1: 5–32.

Larson, B.A. and D.W. Bromley (1990) "Property Rights, Externalities, and Resource Degradation: locating the tragedy", *Journal of Development Economics*, 33(2): 235–62.

Leonard, D.K. and S. Straus (2003) *Africa's Stalled Development: international causes and cures*, Boulder, CO: Lynne Rienner.

Lichtenberg, G.C. (1789), Notebook J.

Lund, C. (2008) *Local Politics and the Dynamics of Property in Africa*, Cambridge: Cambridge University Press.

Macpherson, C.B. (1973) *Democratic Theory: essays in retrieval*, Oxford: Clarendon Press.

—— (1978) *Property: mainstream and critical positions*, Toronto: University of Toronto Press.

Maddison, A. (2007) *Contours of the World Economy, 1–2030 AD*, Oxford: Oxford University Press.

Mankiw, N.G. (2007) *Principles of Economics*, Mason, OH: Thompson South-Western.

Mellor, J. (1990) "Agriculture on the Road to Industrialization", in C.K. Eicher and J.M. Staatz, (eds) *Agricultural Development in the Third World*, Baltimore: Johns Hopkins Press (pp. 70–88).

Meredith, M. (2005) *The State of Africa: a history of fifty years of independence*, London: Free Press.

Merriam-Webster Dictionary, http://www.merriam-webster.com/dictionary/coherence (accessed 29 February 2012).

Migot-Adholla, S., P.B. Hazell, B. Blarel, and F. Place (1991) "Indigenous Land Rights Systems in Sub-Saharan Africa: a constraint on productivity?", *The World Bank Economic Review*, 5(1): 155–75.

Moore, M. (2007) "How Does Taxation Affect the Quality of Governance?", *Tax Notes International*, 47(1): 79–98.

Ndulu, B.J. and S.A. O'Connell (1999) "Governance and Growth in Sub-Saharan Africa", *Journal of Economic Perspectives*, 13(3): 41–66.

Nelson, R.R. and B.N. Sampat (2001) "Making Sense of Economic Institutions as a Factor Shaping Economic Performance", *Journal of Economic Behavior and Organization*, 44: 31–54.

—— and S.G. Winter (1982) *An Evolutionary Theory of Economic Change*, Cambridge: Harvard University Press.

Nunn, N. (2008) "The Long-Term Effects of Africa's Slave Trade", *Quarterly Journal of Economics*, 123(1): 101–37.

Olken, B. and P. Barron (2009) "The Simple Economics of Extortion: evidence from tucking in Aceh", *Journal of Political Economy*, 117(3): 417–52.

Ouedraogo, R.S., J.-P. Sawadogo, V. Stamm, and T. Thombiano (1996) "Tenure, Agricultural Practices and Land Productivity in Burkina Faso: some recent results", *Land Use Policy*, 13(3): 229–32.

Page, T. (1977) *Conservation and Economic Efficiency*, Baltimore: Johns Hopkins University Press.

Pakenham, T. (1991) *The Scramble for Africa: white man's conquest of the dark continent from 1876–1912*, New York: Avon Books.

Peirce, C.S. (ed. by Vincent Tomas) (1957) *Essays in the Philosophy of Science*, New York: Liberal Arts Press.

Place, F. and P. Hazell (1993) "Productivity Effects of Indigenous Land Tenure Systems in Sub-Saharan Africa", *American Journal of Agricultural Economics*, 75: 10–19.

Platteau, J.-P. (1996) "The Evolutionary Theory of Land Rights as Applied to Sub-Saharan Africa: a critical assessment", *Development and Change*, 27(1): 29–86.

Pritchett, L. (1997) "Divergence, Big Time", *Journal of Economic Perspectives*, 11(3): 3–17.

Riddell, R.C. (2007) *Does Foreign Aid Really Work?*, Oxford: Oxford University Press.

Rodrik, D. (ed.) (2003) *In Search of Prosperity*, Princeton: Princeton University Press.

—— (2006) "Goodbye Washington Consensus, Hello Washington Confusion? A Review of the World Bank's *Economic Growth in the 1990s: Learning from a Decade of Reform*", *Journal of Economic Literature*, 44(December): 973–87.

Russell, B. (1945) *A History of Western Philosophy*, New York: Simon & Schuster.

Sachs, J.D. (2005) *The End of Poverty: economic possibilities for our time*, New York: Penguin Press.

—— (2008) *Common Wealth: economics for a crowded planet*, New York: Penguin Books.

—— and A.M. Warner (2001) "Natural Resources and Economic Development: the curse of natural resources", *European Economic Review*, 45: 827–38.

Schumpeter, J. (1961) *The Theory of Economic Development*, New York: Oxford University Press.

Sender, J. (1999) "Africa's Economic Performance: limitations of the current consensus", *Journal of Economic Perspectives*, 13(3): 89–114.

Shackle, G.L.S. (1961) *Decision, Order, and Time in Human Affairs*, Cambridge: Cambridge University Press.

Shleifer, A. and R.W. Vishny (1993) "Corruption", *Quarterly Journal of Economics*, 108(3): 599–617.

Simon, H.A. (1991). "Organizations and Markets", *Journal of Economic Perspectives*, 5(2): 25–44.

Sjaastad, E. and D.W. Bromley (1997) "Indigenous Land Rights in Sub-Saharan Africa: appropriation, security and investment demand", *World Development*, 25(4): 549–62.

—— and D.W. Bromley (2000) "The Prejudices of Property Rights: on individualism, specificity, and security in property regimes", *Development Policy Review*, 18(4): 365–89.

Sugden, R. (1984) "Reciprocity: the supply of public goods through voluntary contributions", *Economic Journal*, 94: 772–87.

Tiffen, M. (2003) "Transition in Sub-Saharan Africa: agriculture, urbanization and income growth", *World Development*, 31(8): 1343–66.

Timmer, C.P. (1990) "The Agricultural Transformation", in C.K. Eicher and J. M. Staatz (eds) *Agricultural Development in the Third World*, Baltimore: Johns Hopkins Press (pp. 47–69).

United Nations Development Programme (UNDP) (2007) *MDG Monitor*, http://www.mdgmonitor.org/ (accessed 5 October 2008).

—— (2010) *The Iraq Briefing Book*, New York: United Nations.

United States Agency for International Development (USAID) (2004) *Policy Reform Lessons Learned*, Washington, D.C.: U.S. Agency for International Development.

van de Walle, N. (2001) *African Economies and the Politics of Permanent Crisis, 1979–1999*, Cambridge, UK: Cambridge University Press.

Walters, C. (1986) *Adaptive Management of Renewable Resources*, New York: Macmillan.

Williams, H. (1977) "Kant's Concept of Property", *Philosophical Quarterly*, 27: 32–40.

Williamson, O.E. (2002) "The Theory of the Firm as Governance Structure: from choice to contract", *Journal of Economic Perspectives*, 16(3): 171–95.

—— (2005) "The Economics of Governance", *American Economic Review*, 95(2): 1–18.

Wittgenstein, L. (1921) *Tractatus Logico-Philosophicus*, 3.05, in A. Kenny (1994) *The Wittgenstein Reader*, Oxford: Blackwell (p. 6).

World Bank (2005a) The Millennium Development Goals, http://www.worldbank.org/ (accessed 10 February 2010).

—— (2005b) *Economic Growth in the 1990s: learning from a decade of reform*, Washington, D.C.: World Bank.

INDEX